The Journey of the Unhealed Child

By Teresa Clifford

Copyright © 2023 by – Teresa Clifford – All Rights Reserved.

It is not legal to reproduce, duplicate, or transmit any part of this document in either electronic means or printed format. Recording of this publication is strictly prohibited.

Table of Contents

Dedication i

Acknowledgments ii

About the Author iii

Chapter 1 Dealing with Crisis in Our Lives 5

Chapter 2 First Steps in Getting to Know My Story 10

Chapter 3 Getting to Grips with Past Memories 16

Chapter 4 The Beginning of My Journey through Therapy ... 23

Chapter 5 No One Can Prepare You for What Will Arise 28

Chapter 6 Times You May Want to Run 32

Chapter 7 The Body Remembers 36

Chapter 8 Healing the Child Within 40

Chapter 9 Understanding Patterns 44

Chapter 10 Dealing with Overwhelming Emotions 46

Chapter 11 Getting to Grips with Remembering 51

Chapter 12 More About Flashbacks 58

Chapter 13 More Memories Arise (Trigger Warning) 61

Chapter 14 Body Talk 66

Chapter 15 Making Sense 69

Chapter 16 Speaking and Remembering Emotions (Trigger Warning) 75

Chapter 17 Mind-set 81

Chapter 18 Boundaries 85

Chapter 19 The Meaning of Love 90

Chapter 20 On Being a Woman 95

Chapter 21 Building Self-Confidence 100

Chapter 22 Learning to Love Yourself After Abuse 104

Chapter 23 Restoring Your Trust in Yourself 109

Chapter 24 Self-Care 112

Chapter 25 Loving Relationships 114

Chapter 26 Knowing Our Patterns 116

Chapter 27 Coming to Terms with Ourselves 120

Epilogue Beginning Anew 125

Resources 130

    Meditation: Healing the Feeling Within 130

    Meditation for Healing the Inner Child 132

    Assertive Ways of Expressing Feelings 136

    Affirmations for Healing from Trauma 136

    My Declaration of Self-Esteem 137

Dedication

With love to my husband for his love and support throughout my healing and to my two children for their steadfast loving presence in my life, which enabled me to continue on my journey towards my healing, and to my five amazing grandchildren.

Acknowledgments

To the volunteer on the other end of the Dublin Rape Crisis Centre, who patiently listened to me, calmed me with her words, and stirred me in the direction of finding the support I needed to begin my journey.

To my first therapist, Una McGuire, for creating a safe space for me to bring my story and to put together the pieces of that story that gave me a deeper understanding of myself and what had happened to me as a child. Una passed some years ago; the legacy she left me with from our time together was one that gave me the courage to continue on my journey towards more self- awareness, self- healing, Self-belief, and the ability to trust in myself more. It was her presence with me in my therapy that made me want to be that presence for another on their journey towards healing.

To all the therapists for over thirty years who continued to help me on my journey towards my personal development, to the trainers who brought out my ability to become a psychotherapist, and to the supervisors for supporting me in my own clinical practice that enabled me to be fully present for the clients that came to me. To you all, I give my thanks.

About the Author

Teresa has worked for over thirty years in the area of healing, psychotherapy, and spiritual coaching. She is a native of Dublin and now lives in Kildare with her husband. She has two adult children and five grandchildren. She has worked as an accredited psychotherapist with the Irish Association of Humanistic & Integrative Psychotherapy for over twenty years. She has helped others work through historical childhood sexual abuse by the Catholic Church and within industrial schools in Ireland and other forms of abuse. She has worked with older people as a facilitator of Ageing With Confidence and has facilitated women's groups in building self-confidence and self- esteem within themselves. The Journey of the Unhealed Child is Teresa's first book, and she hopes that it aids others on their journey towards their healing.

The Journey of the Unhealed Child

A guide to dealing with lost memories of childhood sexual abuse and creating healing from the trauma of remembering.

When I sat down to write this book, I found it difficult to put into words all the learning I have gained over my lifetime thus far. The words I have written within these pages come from my own experiences of remembering and working through childhood sexual abuse. What came out of those experiences and learnings was that there are elements that we all need to heal from any event that brings trauma to our lives. For me, those elements began with having the right kind of support, leading to the understanding that, in turn, helped me to heal. This is my story from my heart to yours in the hope that I can be of support to you on your journey to healing and embracing yourself on your recovery journey.

My longing to be of service to others came from a very young age and became more prevalent when I was in my teenage years. During those teenage years, I held groups for my friends, where I would facilitate them in being honest and open with each other and themselves. This was something I felt passionate about and still do to this day. I wanted to help others to be okay with being themselves and within their relationships.

In later life, the vision grew stronger as I remembered being sexually abused in my childhood and the need to share my learning with others who are going through a similar experience in their lives today.

I have held that vision of bringing insight, learning, and enlightening others by telling my story of my own journey through remembering childhood sexual abuse, sharing my experiences, and the healing I have had within my own life. Teaching others to love themselves and to build loving relationship with themselves and others has been a passion of mine, and it has always been with me. It comes from the spirit I hold within me, and that is within you as well.   After my journey through a breakdown, remembering childhood sexual abuse, my recovery, and the understanding I gained within that journey, I want to bring hope to those of you on a similar journey to aid in the understanding of yourself on your journey and support you towards your healing. I believe that we are all part of God's plan, and when a vision comes to us, it is a calling to grow within ourselves and toward our healing. I feel blessed with the grace of remembering and being able to piece together the healing those memories brought into my life. The trauma of childhood sexual abuse is different for everyone who has been abused in this way. Each one will journey to where their healing resonates with them, and that will be enough for them to find the peace and support they need. Others will go deeper into their process to enable them to be of support to those on a similar path. It is your journey to do it in whatever way is healing for you.

The journey I embarked upon was one of self-reflection, self-knowledge, self-understanding, self-fulfilment, and soul-retrieval of the lost parts of myself and was based on my insights, intuition, and spirituality and from opening my heart as an adult to the heart of the child that lived within me. I hope that, throughout the pages of this book, you will gain a deeper understanding of yourself and, in turn, your own healing.

This is my first attempt to write a book, and it is a calling I have had for many years. And like many of us can be, I was plagued with the thoughts of 'not being good enough. I have learned so much from my own experience of remembering my childhood and the sexual abuse I suffered that then led me on another journey towards studying and becoming a psychotherapist, deepening my knowledge and healing my own life. It also took me on a journey of discovering what lay within my soul as a woman. I want to impart the message that there is healing from childhood sexual abuse.

In telling you my story of how I have overcome the challenges I have faced, I hope that it will help you in your journey to see the beauty of who you are.

We all hold the light of spirit within us. It's part of a bigger energy, God, the Universe, Divine, whatever you choose to call it doesn't matter to me, only that you know that you are part of something bigger than you. I believe that we are all made up of energy, and that energy, for me, is called God. It's the light of our eternal being and resides within our bodies from the day we are conceived. It comes with us through our 40 weeks of gestation into our birth, and within the gestation period, a pattern of energy is being formed for how our lives will span out after we are born. There has been a lot of research into babies remembering this time in the womb and their births. 'Babies Remember Their Birth' by Dr. David Chamberlain was my first introduction to the research behind this theory. My own study on Pre and perinatal psychotherapy has helped me to deepen my understanding of the development of the foetus and the imprints that are made within the energy that is held within the foetus in developing the personality of the baby as it grows. I have experienced my own journey from conception to birth through my training in Pre and perinatal Psychotherapy, and I could identify the imprints that my energy held within the 40-week gestation based on how my mother was throughout her pregnancy and her relationship with my father and herself during the months she carried me.

Throughout the chapters of this book, I hope to relate to you my own experiences and the healing that I underwent to reclaim lost aspects of myself. Not everything I will relate to in the chapters that follow may resonate with you. Only take from what I have written that you can relate to, and my hope is that doing so will help you gain more insights into you as your own person and help you create the healing that is relevant to you on your journey. From my heart to yours, let us begin our journey together.

Chapter 1
Dealing with Crisis in Our Lives

Allowing ourselves to be vulnerable is a courageous act
– Teresa Clifford

In our lives, there are times when we meet a crisis. This crisis can bring us to a place of not knowing where to go or what to do to overcome the crisis and how to heal from it. Everyone's crisis will be different. Within a crisis, we learn to pull on the resilience deep within our being.

My crisis came when I was aged thirty-six years old. The name I gave my crisis was a spiritual emergence from deep within me. I learned to view my crisis like that from the promptings that came from my heart and the search for the love I desired in my life. Yours may come from whatever you are craving in your life and how disruptive your life is at the moment. My crisis began after I had lost both my parents within a year of each other when I was twenty-nine, and seven years later, my life began to spiral downward. It was something that was constantly building in me as I dismissed what I was really feeling and acknowledged what those feelings were relating to me. It came when I felt so overwhelmed that I didn't know how to carry on with my daily life. At first, I didn't understand what was happening to me, how my life had changed since the death of my parents. No one teaches you how to deal with loss and grief. It can be a different process for each of us, depending on the kind of relationship we have with the person we have lost. I had lost my grandfather and an uncle, and their deaths didn't play as big a part in my life as the death of my parents did. Grief is a process that when we lose someone dear to us, it will take as long as it takes for us to come to terms with it based on how we have experienced that loss, the support we have in our lives, and how we interpret the loss for ourselves.

The sudden death of both my parents was difficult for me to come to terms with and something I denied for some time. The overwhelming grief that I felt and had no understanding of how to deal with it other than to try to maintain my life as if my parents were still alive. The denial in me took on the form of taking on the roles they would have had in our family, especially my mother's role. She had played a significant part in the care of her family, as some mothers can do, and somehow, as the eldest, I took over her place with my siblings. She was the carer in our family, and I became that person for my family and friends. I realised later that I had projected onto my friends the need I had for my mother and father to be still part of my life in some way, and over the years after my parent's deaths, I allowed my friends to fill the places my mother and father would have had in my life. In doing this, I was continuing with the belief that they were still with me, and in having this image, I denied my parents' deaths. In filling the void that my parents had left and replacing them with others, I was distracting myself from the fact that my parents weren't there anymore. Denial is part of the journey of trauma before we can fully comprehend what has happened suddenly in our lives. The trauma of losing both my parents so close together had traumatised me and also activated past traumas as well that I had yet to identify. A traumatic event in our lives as adults can ignite other past traumas that have been buried subconsciously in childhood and which we would have held onto and not healed from if they had not been recognised and given the healing needed at those times.

My mother's death was a total shock as she died from a massive heart attack at age fifty-two. We would have expected my dad to die first as he had suffered from emphysema for many years, and my mother cared for him. Even though my dad was in and out of hospital after my mother died, and many times we thought that he would not make it, in the end, his death came as a shock as well.

At the time of my parents' deaths, I could not look at my life. In shock and grief, I lived my life denying how I felt daily. There was a numbness in me, which I now know was caused by their sudden deaths and was a defence I had learnt as a child to deal with the sexual abuse as that child. Seven years after their deaths, my life felt as if it was spiralling out of my control, and it was only when everything fell apart within me and was tumbling down that I was ready to examine my life and how I was creating it. At that time, I felt lost, alone, and unhappy in my life. I now know that when I went into that crisis, I needed to rebuild my life from within myself. A part of me wanted to open up; no matter how hard I tried to shut it down, I couldn't. There was a force greater than me leading me to new understandings and knowledge that would help me create the healing I needed within my life. What I had been taught to believe about myself growing up and how my environment contributed to that belief would come undone as I moved further along my journey.

Where to start building a new foundation within myself was something I had no idea how to begin. The only place to start was to examine what was working for me that brought me happiness and joy and what was creating unhappiness and sorrow for me.

We can all stumble and fall over the rubble of our lives. Sifting through the debris to find what is real, of value, and what has been broken and may need mending if that is possible. When a crisis comes, we have no idea where or how to begin to heal ourselves, only that we need to change our lives to where we really want to be. This is a call that comes from deep within you to guide you to bring more happiness and love into your life.

I learnt that the crisis in my life was the reawakening of my soul, as I believe it to be with any crisis we meet in life. The inner beings we are we bring with us from conception to birth into this physical form, our bodies. Our bodies are the vehicles, the vessels that hold the depth of this eternal aspect of ourselves. They hold a wisdom that is ours alone, yet they are connected to the wisdom of a whole, God, Universe, eternal light, whatever you choose to call it.

We come into this world as the light we are, and throughout our experiences in our mother's womb and in childhood, aspects of that light can be extinguished or dampened down and hidden away. We learned how to be around our parents and other significant adults based on their perceptions of us. We blend into how they wanted us to be, good little girls and boys, and in doing so, our light gets lost at those times. Those around us don't recognize us for the person we are and for our unique way of being that stands out about us. As children, we can hold an inner light, a unique way of being that unless those around us recognise it, encourage it, and develop it; we can learn that we are 'not good enough' just being ourselves. We then adapt to how those who care for us expect us to be.

Life goes on into adulthood. We adapt to others and how they see us and give what they expect of us until it all becomes too much. There comes a time when we realise that the way we live is not attuned to the light we carry inside us. We are now dimming our light with the patterns and beliefs we have learned as children. Then the crisis comes, and we begin to search for ourselves; we question what we have learned from others and the beliefs that others have given us, hoping to find our answers and reclaim the lost parts of ourselves. This is how we can exist within our life, and in doing so, we are recreating all that we have learnt about ourselves from our parents, significant others in our lives, and the environment we grew up in. The good, the bad, and the ugly parts of our learning all mixed together till we become overwhelmed, not knowing who our true self is yet wanting to know 'Who am I really?"

The journey I have taken and my story of that spiritual emergence is what I wanted to share with you. My hope is that as you question who you are, I can support you in reclaiming the lost parts of yourself, bring healing to those parts, and help you gain the trust within yourself to love and understand yourself more with each step. My journey began with the awakening of my inner distress in the form of what others may call a nervous breakdown. The origin I now know came from my childhood and all the unresolved trauma that I had lived with as a child. My sleeping inner child awoke to take me on a journey I had not expected. I struggled to embrace this journey for a while until I knew that my inner child was awakened as part of my healing, and the child in me was bringing me home to the unique light that was within me.

Chapter 2
First Steps in Getting to Know My Story

Taking the time to get to know ourselves is the best way to learn who our true selves are, and in doing so, we can transform our fears and limitations into our own inner power and fill our lives with joy.

- Teresa Clifford

It is by knowing our story and who we are is how we learn to know ourselves. The day we are born is the day our story begins. The beliefs and experiences from our childhood create the adults we become. We are now the heroes of our own lives, and we continue to follow the guidance we had as children, only now we are the adults in our stories. This is the first part of our journey. The second part is when we look at our lives and realise that what we are creating within our lives is not our own desired outcome but something that we are creating from what others taught us to be or wanted us to create. We go in search of ourselves in the hope of creating something more for ourselves than the original story we have carried from childhood.

My story began in the second stage of my life in March 1990, while I was working in a Post Office that I was managing at the time along with the owners of the Post office. The Post Office was within a shop and the premises where the owners resided. This was my first full-time position since I left work after marrying my husband and first having our son and then our daughter three years later. I was a stay-at-home mum for many years and would have taken odd jobs here and there to help subsidize the family income with my husband.

For some time, I felt out of sorts within myself and unsure of where I was. I had panic attacks, which I told no one about and would have carried on each day as if everything in my life was great. Something didn't feel quite right on this particular day in March. I was very agitated and wanted to be far busier than I was that day, so I felt some way in control of my agitation. Keeping myself busy was one of the avoidance patterns I had developed in childhood that helped me deal with my reality as a child. That day was quiet, and there was a panic in me that I found hard to understand or recognize what it was about. This unease continued throughout the day until mid-afternoon when I felt my body shake from head to toe, and I knew then that something was very wrong with me. I felt I needed something to calm the panic and the shaking in my body. I rang my husband and asked him if he could ring the doctor. I described what was happening to me and asked if he could get the doctor to prescribe some medication to help calm me down. There were only a couple of hours left in the day to work. I wanted to continue until the end of the day, as I didn't want anyone to know what was going on with me. This pattern of wanting to hide what was going on in me was something I later learnt was part of the trauma I had been through as a child. As a child, I had held within myself the trauma of being sexually abused because of the fear that had been instilled in me by my abusers of being abandoned by those I loved and that it was something that no one would believe.

An image flashed in my mind as time passed, and it grew closer to going home. It was the image of myself as a young child who was very frightened, and along with that image, the shaking in my body got worse. I found it hard to breathe, and it took all my strength not to run out the door of the Post Office. I was glad now that it was a quiet day and there were very few people about in the Post Office. I don't think I would have been able to control myself in a busy outside world as well as deal with what was happening within me at that time. Closing time came, and another image crossed my mind as I made my way home. The image was me in my bedroom in the dark and someone leaning over me. Somehow, I knew the images and my body's reactions were connected, and as I was driving my car, I shook uncontrollably for some time. I have no recognition of how I made it home. This was the beginning of my memories from my childhood emerging. When I arrived home, my husband told me he had contacted the doctor, who could not give him a prescription without seeing me. At this point, I didn't want to speak any more about what was happening to me, and I fogged off my husband by saying I was okay now. I was far from being okay. I was frantic inside and needed to air what was happening to me. I felt that I couldn't say it to my husband for fear he would think I was going mad. It was something that I feared myself. After seeing how a friend of mine was treated with her depression and mental illness, I didn't want to have a reaction that I couldn't at this point deal with.

That evening, I was going to my brother's house for a drink with my sister-in-law. So again, hiding what was going on for me, I kept to the arrangement. After I had been there for a short while, I blurted out to her what was happening to me and that somehow the images I was seeing and my childhood bedroom were part of it, along with my reaction to those images. Of course, she was shocked, just like I was. Where was all this coming from? Neither of us had the answer at that time. There was an uneasiness in me that I couldn't quite put my finger on. My sister-in-law suggested that I ring someone, a helpline, who may be able to help make some sense of what was happening to me. I decided to do as she said and went home to look up a helpline that may be able to talk to me. I do not recall how I got the Rape Crisis Centre number or why I chose to ring them. It was guidance that came to me from nowhere, or so I thought at the time; I would learn to trust this guidance more throughout my journey. I gave them a call while hiding in the kitchen of our home, hoping my husband wouldn't hear me make the call, as I still found it hard to tell him what was happening to me. Even my actions around how I handled this must seem strange to you, the reader, as I write this. I would later learn that this was another pattern I had from a childhood of hiding away what had happened to me as a child. I was in constant fear as a child, and now it was manifesting in how I was dealing with what was happening when I began to remember something that was in my past.

The woman on the other end of the phone had such a calm and soothing voice that I calmed down and took in what she was saying. She acknowledged that I needed support as something was surfacing for me, and I needed to talk to someone who could help me make sense of what I needed to know. She didn't say everything would be okay straight away, for this was a journey that needed to be taken and that at times it would be painful, yet there was light at the end of the tunnel, and I would be okay. She seemed to have more insight into what was happening without overwhelming me, and I took her direction to make an appointment with a therapist.

After speaking with her and feeling calmer, I told my husband what was happening to me. We drove to the mountains to give ourselves space to talk it through. At this time, I knew that what was happening inside me were insights from something that happened in my childhood, that it had something to do with a presence in my bedroom, and that it felt overwhelming and terrifying. Each time I mentioned the images that were coming to me, my body shook uncontrollably, and I found it hard to breathe. As my husband and I talked, it began to make sense how some of my reactions were unusual in different areas of our relationship. As we talked, I was able to see a light that shone into some of my reactions when we were making love and in other areas of our relationship based on how I would react. Somehow, it made sense that a part of me needed healing and was related to something of a sexual nature that had taken place in my bedroom when I was a child.

My journey began in this way. I believe that our journey toward healing begins at stages in our lives when we become unhappy. It is connecting to that unhappiness that if we allow ourselves to stop and explore this unhappiness, it will lead us to a new way of creating a better life for ourselves. I also believe there are times when those awakenings come that we possess a strength within us at those moments that we didn't have at the time of the traumatic events.

This was only the beginning of the journey. It started for me out of nowhere, or so I thought at the time and became a journey that took many years of insights and brought heartbreak around a childhood I had buried deep inside myself. For those of you who are only starting on a journey of dealing with sexual abuse in your childhood, I hope to create a safe place that aids you on your path toward healing.

By giving you my story, I hope to support you in coming through to the other side of the pain, hurt, anguish, and grief that arises out of facing the demons of childhood sexual abuse. I disassociated from the hurt child in me, pushed her aside, and locked her away deep in my subconscious. I was bringing her back to life again with that first memory. My faith in God, the universe, guides, and angels contributed to a lot of that healing, and I will share with you how their presence in my life aided my healing and the acceptance of a past that had remained hidden in the shadows for far too long. It was in gaining my voice, a voice that was once a whisper that now became a roar for myself and, in time, became a roar for others as my journey progressed. Whoever you are, man, woman, or child, your voice sounds the message that comes from within and lights the way toward your healing. I think children are being heard more today than they were in my time, in the fifties, and this is a good thing. Learning as parents how our own childhoods have impacted us and our ability to parent our own children can help us build stronger, more loving relationships with our children.

Chapter 3
Getting to Grips with Past Memories

Our past can reveal the healing we need today
— Teresa Clifford

Before I even stepped inside the therapy process, my journey had already begun. March was the beginning of remembering, and my first appointment with a therapist was in August. During that time, I would wake up constantly each night with nightmares, and during the day, I was having flashbacks to a past that had evaded me for over thirty years. The windows into my past were frightening and confusing, and I could not make any sense of them. I was terrified of what was happening to me, yet from somewhere deep inside, I sensed guidance from somewhere else within me. I found myself sensitive to the world I was living in. A gesture or a word would trigger me into memories, and I found it hard to know where my reality in the now began and where it ended. It was only later that I realised that the trauma I had been through as a child was now somehow living out in what I was feeling and experiencing as an adult, and it was something I was unable to comprehend at the time fully. I had unknown to myself created my existence in my adult life from my life as a child. I felt that I had regressed into being the child I was back at the time of the abuse, and what I, as the adult, had in her life at the time was the creation of what was abusive from my childhood and lay within my present reality. It is something that I can see now; it was not clear when I was remembering. It felt like I had turned into the distress I was in and associated it with my past as a child and not as something happening to me as an adult. It would begin to make more sense as I moved through my therapy. I was experiencing memories that I had suppressed as a child because I was unable to control or handle what was happening to me, and there were triggers in my adult life that activated those memories for me. What activated these memories in my adult life was how I was in a relationship with the men in my life at the time, the feelings that they activated in me in certain situations, and my reactions to them at those times. Feelings of not being loved, feelings of blame for what was happening within those relationships, feelings of not being in control of my life that others held that control more than me, and feelings of unworthiness of being loved the way I wanted to be loved.

Flashbacks are the term used that are memories from the past and can be frightening when they come. They transported us back to the time of the trauma and existed as if it were happening to us daily. All sense of time and space gets lost as you are transported back to the scenes of the trauma from your childhood. The images, the sensations in your body, and the feelings all come in a rush, and it can be very hard to cope with what is happening to you at the time of the flashbacks. That's where my therapy came into being of support to me when I started it. It enabled me to ground the flashbacks with different techniques, helping me return to the reality of now. It took a lot of practice, but in the end, it was worth it to learn the skills I needed to deal with the trauma of the abuse. It also helped me to understand that there were circumstances in my adult life that were adding to the memories being triggered.

I had an innate instinct to shut myself off and control the flashbacks before getting to therapy. The same instinct naturally comes with protecting you from any trauma. The brain activates the fight-flight-freeze response whenever trauma occurs. It's a natural way of protecting you from harm and bringing safety to you. Whenever trauma reoccurs, it can lock you into the freezing stage, and the instincts that provide you with protection as a child can create problems in your relationships as you grow up. My protection was to shut down and freeze. I could control it this way when I knew I had a date to begin my therapy. I held the therapy space to control what was happening inside of me. I also had friends I could speak with who understood my distress. In the beginning, I was not as discerning about who I spoke with, and I put that down to the fact that after being silent for all those years, I wanted to constantly talk about what was happening to me now as I remembered and also what had happened to me as a child. I was at the time anxious to make sense of what had happened to me and thought that others knew ways of helping me. Seeing my distress only added to their distress, as they had no way of knowing how to deal with what I was saying any more than I did. In time, I learnt that not everyone understood or was willing or able to listen to what I was saying, which added to my distress at the beginning of the process. As the therapist, I will caution those dealing with abuse to look for supportive people until they understand what they are dealing with for themselves. It is important to understand what is happening for you and what has happened to you in childhood and gain the knowledge you need to help yourself be understood and believed.

Those around me found it hard to comprehend what I was saying, and, in them unable to make sense of it with me, it distressed me more and left me feeling that I wasn't believed. I know that no one would be willing to talk about abuse to gain attention, nor would they constantly keep repeating what had happened to them in the hope that they would be believed. I was met with this: I was seeking attention just like I did as a child. There was no way what I was saying was true, and as both my parents were dead at the time, they couldn't collaborate on what I was saying. I was berated for only speaking out after their deaths. I had learnt from my own experience and the experiences of others that speaking out can sometimes only occur when others are dead. It is easier for the person who was abused to speak out then if the form of the abuse was named as love as it was in my life. As a person who has been abused in this way, I found it hard to speak badly of a person who claimed to love me and who I loved. The state of confusion exists from the child who knew love as pain to the adult who learns to keep perceiving love as pain and only stops when the adult begins to question the pain they are in because of what they have learnt as love. It all becomes distorted in the person's mind. This was how it was in my case. My confusion about what love is and was for me battled itself out inside my head as I began to remember more and more of the abuse in my childhood. The denial that I felt when I was asked to explore what I thought love was and to compare it to the love I was shown as a child became a constant battle in me at the beginning of my therapy, and yet somewhere deep inside of me, I knew what the true answers were.

When I looked back on that day in March 1990, I saw it as a breakthrough, a spiritual awakening; others may see it as a breakdown. If I had seen it as a breakdown, I would have ended up in psychiatric care and on medication. I chose to see it as a gift for most of my journey, an insight that needed investigation, a piecing together of a puzzle that was my sheltered life, and I felt blessed to have these insights that led me to find a more natural way of dealing with what I remembered because of how unnatural I felt my life had been as a child; now, as an adult, I saw how aspects of my childhood were due to sexual abuse. The insights I was given were coming from deep within me. I believe the insights were God's way of directing me toward healing.

The only way to describe the fragmented parts of myself is to ask you to recall a movie you have seen where a tragic accident or tragic event leaves the person without the memory of that event. It's called amnesia. It's the brain's way of protecting the person from feeling and remembering something so shocking that they cannot take in the event as it is. Over time, snippets of the tragedy begin to seep through, and the person regains their memory when they are in a place to handle it.

For years, I would have had similar snippets that didn't make sense, and I would dismiss them. I didn't at the time know how to interpret them because, as a child, I lacked the understanding or knowledge to make sense of them. Also, I had learnt to dismiss them in how my parents taught me how they dealt with aspects of their own lives. So, if you are like me as you begin your journey and are starting to remember in snippets, and it frustrates you as it did me that I didn't have the full answer, have patience with yourself. Your brain has protected you for a reason, knowing the right time to allow the pieces to fall into place. You may need more knowledge to understand something or even have other experiences that will help you gain the knowledge you need. It's trusting that all will be revealed when it is ready to be revealed and that forces are working to support you in the best way possible toward the healing you need.

As a child, I was always aware of others around me that came not so much as an image but more as an energy, a feeling of being held, and the warmth that came to me from that feeling. I would try to put images on them, and sometimes, I would stop the energy they sent towards me. In my darkest hours as a child, I felt the presence of that light surrounding me and bringing calmness to me by taking me out of my body, away from the experience of being abused. From outside of my body, I would watch what was happening to me from above my body. There were times when I would be brought further beyond the room I was in into another realm with light, a wonderful sense of peace and calm.

I am sharing my story, my journey, practices, and spirituality throughout the following chapters. In this opening chapter, I have shared how it began with insights into how a breakthrough can occur. A thought or an image comes to mind that doesn't seem to make any sense, and it is dismissed. How I would have thought it had come out of nowhere. Only as I processed the memories did I realise that over the years, snippets were emerging, and I would have closed them down. There was a process going on before my full awakening. That process was what I had experienced throughout my life up to the point of remembering. It all added to my awakening of why my life wasn't the way I wanted it to be—seeing that I was automatically going through my life and had been that way since I was a child. Never questioning how or why I was living my life the way I was, just going through the motions was how I dealt with my life from childhood till the point of my remembering—not knowing that there was a part of me that lay in the shadows until I had gained my first insight that I had been sexually abused me as a child.

I truly believe that there is a force that comes with us into this life when we are born. Some of us may call that force your guardian angel; others may call it something else. I believe I chose my parents and others on a soul level to come to for the learning I needed in this lifetime. I had all the knowledge I needed before my birth of what I would need throughout my life that would come to me and help me make sense of my life and guide me to those who could help me to understand more than my parents could ever have. There was guidance in my life, and I struggled to trust it, to see it as someone or something bringing me home to myself. My parents laid the foundation of my life that was solid in parts and rocky in others. The loyalty I held for them at the time was the struggle to see that some of the foundations they had laid were rocky ones, and I needed to learn to lay down new foundations in these areas that would bring me home to myself.

So, wherever you are in your journey, I hope you will journey further with me as I unfold more of my story. I wish that, in some way, I can be of service and support to you as we journey together throughout the chapters and pages of this book.

Chapter 4
The Beginning of My Journey through Therapy

Reach inside and touch your soul; there lies the beauty that you seek.

– Teresa Clifford

At the beginning of therapy, I was dealing with some memories of being abused by a member of my family. Memories that came in the form of nightmares, feelings, and sensations in my body and the anxiety I would feel around others. Some of the memories I knew now were real, like the image of someone leaning over me in the dark in my bedroom, which was clearer now than when I had begun to remember. Other images and memories began to emerge around being abused by another member of my family; this had a different feel to it than the first memories I had. The original first memory was around an incident that happened to me around the age of eight, whereas the memories that were coming to me now where of images of me being younger and the abuse being ongoing and regular. Sometimes, the first memories that come to us are the ones that are paving the way for other memories to arise. The memories that came to me left me feeling that I was always under someone else control rather than my own. The struggle I felt trying to come to terms with all the images that were presenting themselves to me, all the sensations and feelings that went along with those memories felt unreal at times. The second memories that came to me had a reality to them that felt abusive to my need of not wanting to partake in the abuse that was happening to me. It felt like an unreal situation and a different kind of abuse than what I first began to remember. The change that came over this family member was something that frightened me. A different side of them emerged, and a different personality came to the fore. Even thinking back now brings shivers to me of how hard it was to comprehend that this was something that was happening to me and, in my abuser's words, 'this was love.' It didn't feel like love at the time, nor after it happened. My abuser would beret me for making him ask me to do what he wanted me to do to him and who he was with me. It was all my fault. I grew up believing that whatever happened in my relationships with others was always my fault and that I had done something to make that person react to me the way they did.

As children, we see the adults around us as the authority in our lives, and we follow what they say, believing that they have our best interests at heart. We never question them; even if we did, we would not have the full knowledge or experience to fully understand that they may not be the ones we can trust.

The day I arrived for my first session with the therapist that had been recommended to me, I can easily say I was terrified, both the child in me that was awakening and the adult in me who had no idea how to cope with what had happened to the child or what was happening to me now in my life. It was like I was leading myself as a child by the hand to figure out how we would both deal with what had happened to her and what was happening to me simultaneously. I felt the split within me; it was like we were two different people, yet we were connected. One could not heal without the other.

The first session in therapy is more about updating the therapist on what is happening to you and a little about your background. It may feel hard at times to focus on having what seems like a normal introduction to another because of all that is going on for you. I know all I wanted to do was scream at her to help me. If I could have gotten a quick answer, I would have taken it then and there. The one thing about going into therapy is that you may have the idea that it will be a quick fix and that things will get back to normal or the way they were before the memories came in. It was what I thought at the time. I thought a few sessions and I would have this all figured out. It took several sessions and even years to grasp all I needed to know and work through fully. I was glad that my therapist at the time could be realistic with me and asked me to come for at least six weekly sessions to see how we could work together.

It is important for you as a client to feel at ease or at least comfortable with the person you have chosen as your therapist. It is a relationship, and your past relationships have caused the pain you now may find yourself in. I had chosen a female therapist because I was uncomfortable with a male therapist. That would come later on in my journey. I wanted to come from my voice this time as I was so used to listening to the opinions of others, especially the males in my life, that I lost my voice at times. This was relevant to how I was brought up, how I was taught to listen more to how my father was the main authority for us, and how he dictated how things were in our home. He was the one who had most of the say in how we were to behave and conduct ourselves.

As children, we are like sponges. We take in all that is around us in our environment, what our parents and other adults tell us, and how they behave towards us. We trust without question, and when we do get to question, our questions may not be received the way we can get the answers we need, or they may be dismissed. So much wasn't part of me, yet I carried it for years. All the blame, the belief that I was bad and that no one could love me, that I wasn't strong or clever enough, and that I wasn't enough in anything I tried to be or do.

Trauma is the problem, not you. Every pattern, every belief, and every coping mechanism that developed in you is from the shock and trauma you have been through as a child and was a natural response to your experience of sexual abuse in your childhood. Our brain is wired to keep us safe, so in the case of trauma, your brain is working to protect you from the traumatic event. When that event reoccurs, your brain gets wired to deal with it protectively. Until you acknowledge and understand what has happened to you and the coping mechanisms that came into place for you, it is only then that you can begin to relate to how to heal from it and build a bridge to reclaim the lost parts of yourself.

To protect yourself from traumatic events, you learn to disassociate from what is happening to you. You may leave your body; your mind may fixate on something within the room. You numb yourself from feeling the pain of the trauma and store it away in parts of your brain that, with the protection, you can have no memory of what has happened as it is too overwhelming for you to comprehend as a child. It can even happen to you as an adult when something traumatic happens. Your brain stores the trauma away and develops the patterns you need to survive.

I had no idea that the patterns and mechanisms of my childhood trauma were affecting my life as an adult, as I had shut myself off from what was happening to me at the time of the abuse. It was only within my relationships as an adult that I began to question why I felt so hurt all the time in my relationships. In asking that question, the answers began to come to me. I am a great believer that there is a God, and when the time is right, when we have had all the experiences we need, and when we question our lives, it is then that the answers come to us. I feel that every part of my life and my adult experiences was telling the story of how I had experienced my childhood. That's what I felt was happening to me as I began to remember my childhood. It felt like both my childhood and adulthood were as one, and as of yet, I was unable to distinguish that there were some differences between them.

My faith was strong, and in the first memory, I knew deep inside me that what came as a thought was a door opening up into the disassociated part of myself. I had opened the door, and my child invited me into her world.

She wasn't yet ready to be fully in my world at the beginning until I found a safe place for her to be present, and that was with me in therapy. So, our journey began. To heal from the trauma, we first need to build a safe and supportive environment to begin dealing with childhood sexual abuse. That will take as long as it takes. You must have a safe place and support to deal with the trauma before going deeper into it. Living your daily life and managing the symptoms of that trauma will help you feel the safety and support you need to heal. My therapy became that for me and where I learnt how to create a safe environment and support myself.

Chapter 5
No One Can Prepare You for What Will Arise

The light we carry within our souls is the bridge we need to create a better self and, in turn, a better life for us.

- Teresa Clifford

As much as you can try to prepare yourself for each session of therapy, you will come away with new insights and new understanding. Painful and scary, even though they can be at times, you will know somewhere inside you are healing. The beginning for me was a thought, then images of dreams, flashbacks, body sensations, and the overwhelming sense of emotions that everything I was experiencing was true. Sometimes, I felt frantic, wanting it to be over quickly, wanting to run away and take flight as I did as a child. The trauma was happening again, but now, with a consciousness of the experiences of the adult, I was.

Every fear and uncomfortable feeling I would have in a physical or sexual relationship helped to give the answers to what had happened to me as a child. In all my relationships, the child in me was crying out to be heard, and I had no way of listening to her and everything she was telling me. I didn't understand what a healthy, loving relationship was. My understanding of a loving relationship was distorted by what had happened to me as a child.

It's not easy to face the reality that you were abused by those you loved and thought they loved you. There is no way a child can distinguish what love is for themselves if they haven't been given insights into what love is. The love you carry inside of you is the love you were taught as a child. Not until our lives are in turmoil do we reach out for the real meaning of love and where it is in our lives as adults.

It's hard to describe the deep sadness of knowing that a relative I loved had abused me at a young age and that another relative had done the same at a different age. When I first entered therapy, I was bringing in the abuse that had happened to me at around eight years of age, and then, later on, uncovered the abuse that happened to me at a younger age. The abuse that happened to me at a younger age was what I found the most difficult to deal with. The world I had built around my abuser fell asunder, and my world as an adult fell apart with my family, too. There were times I wanted to leave, to run away, yet I knew that this was what I had done as a child to keep me safe. I hid somewhere deep inside of me. I wasn't facing my abusers; I was facing myself on behalf of the child I was and learning to love her as she hadn't been loved before.

There is resistance within all of us at times of crisis, and you will meet resistance from your family of origin should you choose to tell them about what it is you remember, especially if it relates to family members. I knew my head was all over the place with what was coming up for me, and I needed to talk to the rest of my family to try and make sense of what I was remembering. It was a mistake on my part because I felt more isolated and alone by their reactions, and I felt that I was going mad at the time, whereas I was becoming saner than I had ever been before, remembering.

As a therapist now, I would always work through with my clients their expectations around telling someone close to them about their abuse and even to their family members. My therapist at the time didn't work through this part of my healing with me.

Support is really important to a person going through remembering childhood sexual abuse. I had no recollection of it until I began to recall what had happened to me that day in March with that first memory and when the flooding of images and sensations came rushing in. What I remembered were not false memories or suggested in therapy. They were there before I stepped into therapy. Therapy helped me to piece together and recollect what I was remembering and to make sense of all those events through how I experienced my life as an adult. For those who do remember and speak out about their childhood sexual abuse for the first time, it is important to choose someone you trust to listen and believe you. Support from a person other than just the therapist makes the healing much more powerful for the person speaking about their experiences and the impact it has had on them. The response of being believed is really important. I know I wasn't believed at first, and I know how that impacted me. No one talks about abuse if it is something they haven't experienced. I suppose in seeking out my family's support and seeking answers, I doubted myself as much as they were of me. Looking back now, it was more important that I believed in myself and gave myself the time to come to my beliefs about what had happened to me. Instead, I turned to my family, who had no answers for me, and then my belief in myself, the little I had, began to waver. This was part of a pattern that was caused by the abuse, too. The coping that would have been installed in me as a child by my abusers. I would be made to believe that it was something that hadn't happened to me by my abusers. It was something I was creating that made it my fault that it had happened. Therefore, I felt it was my fault for how my family reacted to me. I had yet to build up my belief in myself, which today is stronger than it would have been back when I first began remembering.

I recommend you do this at the beginning of your journey. Check out how you envisage telling someone about your abuse and how you see their reaction to what you are saying. It would have been important for me to feel stronger in my understanding and belief before I spoke to another about it. It didn't work for me that way. I was frantic about what I was remembering, as I felt that it was coming out of a dark, hidden place to someone who does remember throughout their lives. From my practice as a therapist, I have learned that remembering the abuse is different from having it suddenly come out of nowhere. When you have no recollection of being abused, it is harder to make sense or comprehend where it is coming from and why it arises when it does. My abuse happened from a very young age and became a normal part of my life for many years. It felt normal until I realised it wasn't, and how I acted out was not a normal way of being.

Chapter 6
Times You May Want to Run

Facing our fears and challenging them is how
we learn to bring our light into the world.
- Teresa Clifford

Taking on this journey is no easy task. I felt I had no choice but to be on this journey if I wanted to heal my life. To heal, I needed to work through what was happening within me and around me. In hindsight, I am sorry I told my family when I was amidst the turmoil. Being in that place, I felt I created more turmoil around me. Had I waited till I felt more in control of what was happening to me, I would not have felt guilty for the upset I caused to those in my family who were as shocked as me by what I was saying. I shared my shock of remembering with them in the hope that I would receive their support in putting the pieces of my memory together.

Yes, there were times when what I remembered was the same as others in my family about part of how our family was and especially how our parents were within the family. However, no one could connect with the abuse. I seemed to be the only one with memories of being abused. I have yet to understand why that was, and it sometimes left me feeling hateful towards being female. I was the only female child in my family for the first eight years of my life, and during these eight years, my abuse happened. As I write this, I can feel the fear that comes with those eight years of being the only female child in our family and how I was treated.

To the outside world, everyone saw me as a doting young child. I didn't feel like that at the time. I felt isolated from my siblings, and the more I was seen as special by my abuser, the more isolated I became with each passing year. I felt I didn't belong and went out of my way to adapt to what was happening to me. I wanted to feel safe and secure and to belong within my family. As a child, I would explode with anger and frustration and soon learnt that it wasn't safe to express these feelings. I would numb myself from feeling all these emotions because I felt overwhelmed by having them and staying safe.

I used to beat myself up for not remembering or speaking out. I felt that I should have been able to stop it and somehow done something different. I later realised the child in me helped me survive. I used everything in my power as that child to adapt to the situation I was in, and my brain helped me to create ways of adapting and surviving the trauma of being abused. I realised as a child; I did what I could to save myself, survive the abuse, and protect myself from being hurt too much. What I learnt about survival as a child didn't serve me as an adult. The same survival only created more hurt for me as an adult. I saw danger all around me. I couldn't recognise when I was truly loved and when I was being hurt. It was all mixed up in a melting pot, and it was hard for me to be discerning when I was being treated lovingly and when I was being treated badly.

In the first year of my therapy, I was numb at times and flooded with overwhelming feelings at other times. I felt like I was on a roller-coaster. My moods shifted and changed so much within that year. I had to learn how to feel and identify and find my feelings' names. As a child, if those around us can feel and understand what they feel, then we will learn how to feel and manage our emotions. When those around us don't acknowledge or even know what they are feeling, we cannot learn how to hold, soothe, and ease our emotions.

Emotions that are locked in our bodies need motion. They need to be expressed, or they manifest as illnesses in our bodies. During my first months of therapy, I felt all I was doing was expressing my anger and frustrations at what had happened to me as a child. I took bio-energy classes where I was taught to listen to the tension in my body, identify the emotion within the tension, and give it expression. At first, it was all about just being able to release the tension of emotion and not wanting to deal fully with it. That constantly happened in my sessions with my therapist and the bio-energy classes. As I gained more insight and understanding of what I was dealing with and its impact on me, other emotions rose to the surface. Grief and sadness surfaced, and this took some time to process. There was a shift from anger and frustration to grief and sadness. It felt like I had to strip away these emotions to reach deeper into the well of good feelings that lay beneath it all.

The process of therapy is like a dance. You step in and out of different emotions, and soon, you begin to recognise that there is more to you than just the memories of the abuse. The buried feelings of joy, laughter, love, and pleasure lay buried within me because allowing myself to feel them would, as a child, have brought an onslaught of more hurt and pain because, as a female, I was taught that I didn't have a right to these feelings as they were a sin against God. Joy, laughter, and love didn't come into the religion I learnt about. It was more about control, fear, and damnation. I learnt to fear the feelings of joy, laughter, and love from the confusion of being told by my parents their interpretation of these feelings and how uncomfortable they felt with these feelings. There is so much that I was taught to misunderstand about love in relationships by both of my parents. As parents and adults, we will carry what we have been taught about relationships in how our parents treated each other and us. It is in exploring our relationship with our parents and other significant adults in our lives as children that we begin to know and understand the kind of love and understanding we need to heal ourselves.

Chapter 7
The Body Remembers

Our bodies hold the messages that we sometimes want to forget or ignore.
– Teresa Clifford

The first book recommended to me at the beginning of my journey was *'You Can Heal Your Life* by Louise Hay. It became my go-to resource as I worked through my therapy, which has a body-centered approach to accessing the memories coming up for me as I began my journey toward healing from the trauma of my childhood sexual abuse.

Louise connected the body, mind, and emotions I was so split from. When abuse happens to us, we can split from our emotions and separate from our bodies. My body would have reactions that my mind couldn't comprehend, and my emotions created a chain reaction in both my mind and my body. With the help of Louise's book, I learned to listen to my body, how it spoke to me, and the messages it was sending me. When I connected with my body, the images that came as flashbacks began to connect with the sensations I was experiencing within my body, it was hard at times to feel, relate to my body's sensations, and know that each one was telling my story for me. It took a while for my mind to piece all of it together. It was like a puzzle, trying to find the right image, match the emotion, and then with the sensations in my body. To place each piece with what my mind knew with the unforgotten parts that had laid dormant for many years.

Going back to those first steps and remembering how distressing they were and my disbelief that this had happened to me was as confusing for me as it was for those I lived with. All of us were trying to make sense of what was happening to me, and yet, somehow, there was a truth arising out of all the confusion. My husband had always sensed something had happened to me as a child but could never put his finger on it directly. Only as my story began to unfold things made sense to him and me.

There was anger and frustration in the beginning. There were times when I wanted to run away from it all, times I felt that I would go mad with all the images that kept coming forth. The struggle and tiredness came with trying to live each day as best I could to be there for my children, go to work, and keep a home. Looking back now, I know I expected so much of myself because of the guilt I felt in being the way I was and the upset I was bringing into our lives.

The beginning of anything new is hard. We need the support of others who have the skills or have been through something themselves and have healed to sit with another person and be with them in their struggle and pain. I felt blessed to have had those people in my life for most of my journey. There were times when, in my urgency to release myself from my pain, I would have gone to other therapies without fully knowing what they were about, just in the desperation to relieve my suffering.

I soon learnt that the only way to heal the pain was to lean into it. To listen to it, acknowledge it, see it, and be present with it. That's what I received from the therapist I was attending. Her gentle presence, hearing and seeing me, helped me to do the same for myself.

The process of remembering and taking steps toward healing is sometimes difficult. All I can say is that it is worthwhile, and there is light at the end. Understanding that there has been trauma in your life and the trauma caused the problem, not how you coped with it. The survival methods that came out of that trauma were natural responses to the events that happened to you. Knowing how our brains work and how our instincts kick in to keep us safe and help us survive the trauma we have been through can help us build the bridge needed for our healing.

I have learnt many techniques and gained skills and knowledge that helped me heal from my childhood sexual abuse trauma. Everyone's trauma is different; how our brains and instincts kick in to help us survive the trauma is natural to all when we are threatened and feel unsafe. Understanding how we process trauma is where the beginning of healing starts.

When I came to a point where my life and how I was living it was causing me pain, that's when the sleeping child within me began to stir, to awake, and to bring the knowledge and information I needed to heal my life. The child within me led me to seek support and find a therapist, and it was in allowing the sleeping child in me to awaken that I found a wholeness within myself that enabled me to embrace myself as a child and as an adult. The void that kept my split from the child within me was filled with the first memory that came to me as a child and kept being filled with each consecutive memory that followed. The understanding that Louise Hay's book brought me helped me understand the messages that my body was sending me. How to integrate them within my mind opened the door to connecting more with my truth, soul, and spirit and set me free from the misbeliefs I had gathered and lived from my childhood about myself and my world.

Later on in my life, I learnt from other books, too. Babette Rothschild's book *'The Body Remembers'* brought further insight into the deeper impacts of trauma on the body and the mind and helped deepen my understanding and healing. In turn, the healing I can bring to others. I took part in Babette's trauma training as well, which brought me the skills and techniques I needed to work with others in their trauma to help them bridge the gap that the untreated trauma left in their lives, from feeling unsafe to finding safety in their lives today. It also gave me great insights into how to process my trauma more.

Chapter 8
Healing the Child Within

There's a wounded child within us all guiding us towards the healing we need when we make the time to connect with that part of ourselves
— Teresa Clifford

As I mentioned earlier, when I first entered therapy, I imagined myself as an adult bringing a wounded child by the hand, looking for healing and support for us both. I had no idea when my journey started how I would be able to help my child; I only knew that I needed someone to help me to help her. I was so separate from her at the time that I didn't realise that I was also looking for the help and support I needed to heal. We were both part of the other, yet we had kept our distance from each other for many years, neither feeling safe to reveal ourselves to the other or anyone else. Then the time came when I couldn't live how I was, and in looking for the answer to my unhappiness and the lack of love I felt in my life, I permitted her to wake up and to be my guide towards the healing we both needed to create a better more loving life from now on. I felt I had taken on the role of a parent holding their child's hand, knowing that their child was hurting and that, in turn, caused the parent to hurt as well as the parent had no way of easing the pain for either of them.

My journey all began with a 'WHY.' Why was I hurting so much in my relationships? Why did I not like who I was? Why was I always longing to be someone else, to be somewhere else? WHY? Sometimes, we ask the question, and we want to know the answer. Sometimes, we get the answer, and we resist it. For me, it was a process of wanting to know and resisting the knowledge coming with the answers I needed. The avoidance of the pain and the exhilaration of having the answers I needed. The answers ebbed and flowed within me. The excitement of having a reason that made sense of how I was in my life brought an understanding of the pain I was in, and then facing the overwhelming pain that came with the answers was something I struggled with and was hard for me to deal with at the time.

It was like the merging of two parts of me. The part of me that thought my life felt perfect as a child and the part of me as an adult whose life was falling apart. It was like a battle between how I was feeling inside and how I was presenting myself to the world around me. The two parts were in constant battle with each other. I would relate it to a screaming child who was hurting and looking for someone to take the pain away and being ignored by an adult or the adult shutting her down and telling her to be quiet. The only person doing this to me at the time was me.

The more I quieted the scream inside of me, the stronger it became until there was no keeping it quiet anymore. Images flooded my mind, overwhelming me until I began to talk about what was happening to me. I had opened a door that I had closed long ago. I was too frightened as a child to speak about what was happening to me, and I lacked the knowledge to say what I wanted to say as that child and then as an adult, having no comprehension or awareness of what sexual abuse was. The adult was learning what was real and not real and was beginning to make sense of it and, in turn, taught the child to tell her story, my story. We did it together with the help and support of those who had gone before us and from those who had researched and learnt the skills needed to heal us both.

Childhood sexual abuse impacts all aspects of the child and, later on, the adult that the child becomes. The strategies you learn to survive as a child you learnt were normal to help you cope with the trauma of the abuse. There were times when I felt less than normal in my life, especially when I looked around and could see a different family image of others than the one I had for myself. It wasn't that others had a perfect family; it was the way they could be so real with each other while I presented an image of my family that was perfect, therefore hiding the secrets behind the front door of our childhood home. Not to mention the arguments, the disagreements, and the punishments, all held within the walls of our home. I know for me, as a child, I dare not speak about our family outside of those walls and that front door. These are my memories, and the rest of my family may hold different ones from me. This is my story about my own life within that family and how I came to heal myself from the unmentioned and unresolved things that happened to me.

There are happy memories as well as a child. The trips we took as a family to visit different places in Ireland for holidays, the days out with my mum's family and all the cousins spending time and playing together, an extension of my own family, and yet in all of this, I felt separated and disconnected, unable to engage and enjoy these times to their fullest fully. It is something that now, as an adult, I can fully immerse myself in, especially with my children and grandchildren.

It is a hard journey to step out on, yet rewarding. Sometimes, within the darkness, I would focus on a glimmer of light ahead that called me forward. I would have done this as a child, too, for I always had my angels and guides with me. It was to these that I spoke to and listened to for their advice on what to do. Through my journaling and meditation, I can still feel their presence and guidance coming through for me. As a child, I would have had an imaginary friend. I know I could relate to this friend as an angel or guide or someone I admired at the time, like Joan of Arc, who dared to speak out for justice and truth and become a warrior for those vulnerable in her society.

What is it I want to impart to you, my reader? Each of us has a journey, our journey. We may cross paths with others who can relate to parts of our journey. For each of us, there is a part that will be unique to us, and from this part, our light will arise with insights, understanding, knowledge, and compassion so that we become the heart and soul of our unique light.

Chapter 9
Understanding Patterns

Our life experiences weave patterns in us, and those patterns either serve us or create harm to us

– Teresa Clifford

They say patterns carry on through the generations until someone dares to question what those patterns mean for them and their lives. I remember being told a story of a young girl watching her mother cook a ham at Christmas and asking her mother why she cooked one half of the ham on the top of the cooker and the other in the oven of the cooker. Her mother replied that it was the way her mother did it. The young girl, still curious, went to her grandmother and asked her the same question, and the grandmother answered that it was the way her mother cooked the ham. Still curious, the young girl went to her great-grandmother and asked the same question, and her great-grandmother replied. I don't know why your mother and grandmother do it that way. I cooked it that way because I couldn't fit the whole ham into my pot. Sometimes, traditions are not what they seem. We can carry on doing things the way our parents and grandparents did and never question the reasoning behind the patterns or traditions.

There are patterns we carry on regarding how we relate to others that our parents have taught us, and they, in turn, have been taught by their parents. In questioning some of those patterns, we learn to become more of our authentic selves. Some of the patterns you will carry on will bring you joy and happiness, and others you need to question, especially those that bring you down, pain, and upset.

When trauma happens to us as children or adults, our brains send messages to protect us. We go into fight, flight, freeze, or fawn mode, depending on the trauma we are experiencing.

To understand how you are each day, you need to know what uplifts you and what pulls you down. When you do more of what is uplifting for you, this is when you know you are living with your authentic self and that you are also listening to the whispers and callings of your soul. The callings from your soul are always leading you to a happier, more loving life. The soul's callings bring expansion. The messages that come as discontent in your life are your soul's way of telling you to heal and reach beyond where you are right now in your life. It tells you there is more for you than you can even begin to comprehend.

Chapter 10
Dealing with Overwhelming Emotions

At the start of any journey, we can experience overwhelming emotions. The journey through childhood sexual abuse comes with emotions that we haven't allowed ourselves to feel at the time of the abuse for fear of being hurt even more. When we begin to remember and connect with certain emotions we have had throughout our lives as an adult, we gain insights from experiencing these emotions, which in turn connects us with a way of beginning to understand these emotions and how they relate to what we felt inside as a child. The emotions I felt were familiar to me at the time of the abuse. They were so familiar that I didn't want to feel them, or I would try as I had before to push them away or distract me from them. They would only come back stronger and overflow into my daily life, where the smallest thing would set me off, and I would be so sensitive to a comment or gesture that another made towards me or another.

The sensitivity I felt at the time was like an open wound that was festering and painful with no way of getting it healed or soothed. This happens when our feelings are not recognised, listened to, or felt both by ourselves and others. Not everyone can deal with their emotions, even more so when you are not dealing with them yourself.

The first thing that is needed from you is to acknowledge and accept that you are feeling what you are feeling. The more you push it away or deny the feeling or feelings, the more you continue to be in pain. By accepting the feelings and allowing yourself to sit with them, the more the answers to healing those feelings and emotions come about.

When we experience emotions that we are uncomfortable with, we have two ways of dealing with them. We either shut them down, hold them back, or express them, giving credence to what we feel. It gives our emotions a sense of flow when we express them. In doing so, it can bring about a deeper understanding of the message they are relating to us about where we are in relationship to those in our lives or to our thought process that is creating what we are feeling and where it would have originated in our lives.

Feelings never lie. They help us with what is nurturing us or what is being taken from us. When someone pressures us to feel something we are not feeling, we tend to think that something is wrong with us. We are told 'we should be happy, 'we should be grateful, and all that we should be is based on others' expectations of us, and maybe that is not how you may see yourself. We are told as children that we 'should be good girls and boys and are given a set of rules to follow based on others' perception of what good means. Maybe we are told not to question things or others' behaviours and to get on with it and rewarded when we do. We are being taught to deny our true selves and continue to do that throughout our adult lives until something or someone makes us question how we are in our lives. It can open the doors to more exploration of what it means to be true to ourselves.

This was my experience on my journey. I was following the rules my parents had set out for me, making me think I was happy with my life. Letting anyone know my true feelings felt like betraying what my parents had taught me. While all the time, I was betraying myself as I had been betrayed as a child. The perfect family was the mask I was taught to wear to be the 'good little girl.' What was hidden behind that mask was all the pain and suffering I experienced as a child, and now, as an adult, I was experiencing it, too. Please don't get me wrong. There was good within my family, too. At the beginning of my remembering, I could not see that the abuse was the pain of what was left unhealed. It overtook the good within my family. In ways, my parents were like any parents of their time. They struggled to keep a roof over their family's heads, put food on the table, and clothe and educate their children. That was the normality that covered up what wasn't the norm within the relationship between parent and child.

There comes a time in our lives when we ask, 'Is what I have learnt about myself as a child my truth or a truth that I learnt from how others saw me and wanted me to be.' I know when I began to question and explore this for myself, I learnt that I avoided my feelings of not being loved, not being heard or seen, and I pushed them away in the same way that they had been pushed away in my childhood.

So, with each thought you have about yourself, it is important to seek out the truth. Is it your voice you hear or another's? Is this something you have learnt to say to yourself, and if so, is it helpful, or is it destructive towards you loving yourself? What feeds your soul? What lights you up? When we control how we feel and think about ourselves, we allow ourselves to be our true selves. We can be vulnerable in speaking our truth, yet in doing so, we find that our vulnerability can become our strength, too. By knowing what's good about ourselves, we can feed that aspect of ourselves more, building our confidence in those areas of our lives. By acknowledging what we feel is not so good about ourselves, we can take the pressure off ourselves in trying to be what we are not and know that in doing so, we can work on building more strength in these areas of our lives.

Knowing what feelings we are comfortable with and the ones we are not helps us lean more into the uncomfortable ones, acknowledge them, and seek to find the answers to the messages those feelings bring us. It may be something that you need support with. I know it was something I needed in my own life when I felt the overwhelming emotions I felt in remembering my childhood experience. Every feeling we have holds a message for us. Sadness shows us how much we care. Anger gives us the message that we need freedom from what is hurting or upsetting us in our lives. Joy helps us know what makes us happy. Each feeling tells us our story, and embracing it can help us find our way to create a better life for ourselves.

- What emotions do you feel comfortable feeling?
- What emotions do you feel uncomfortable feeling?
- How did those around you treat your feelings? Were they embraced or ignored?
- What feelings were embraced, and what ones were ignored?

Write the answers to these questions in a journal and allow yourself to feel how they sit with you and what they bring up for you. Are they showing you areas where you are dismissing your feelings, and can you see the impact that dismissing them has on your life?

BE gentle with yourself with whatever arises, and do the meditation in the resource section to help heal what has come up for you.

Chapter 11
Getting to Grips with Remembering

HEALING DEFINITION *'The process of making or becoming sound or healthy again.'*

How do we know when or what we need healing for? Outside of ourselves, we measure ourselves by how others are or what they think of us. I lost sight of myself, especially in times of distress. I now know that my experiences in childhood defined how I viewed my world in later life as an adult. There came a point in my life when I was feeling off in my relationships and noticed that there seemed to be a difference between myself and others in how I was relating to the men and the women in my life. I began to question why I was that way, both in how I was being treated and how I treated others. This was a very painful time for me as I didn't fully understand where I was in myself, why I was hurting in my relationship, and why I was acting as I was. I hid from my true feelings, and the more I did this, the more I made it worse. This was something that I had been taught as a child to deny what I was feeling during the abuse. When I remembered, I didn't realise that I was still using the patterns I had learnt as a child to survive and manage my life. They were not working for me anymore in my adult life. If anything, they were recreating the pain and hurt that I had experienced in childhood.

What I had experienced more prominently in my mid-thirties was the catalyst for the healing I needed to begin. My life was spinning out of my control. I now know I was still dealing with my life from what I had learnt from being abused as a child. How I was in my life at that time was telling its own story of how I wasn't in control of my life in the way I wanted to be. Like that child, I wasn't in control of her life. I began to feel that I was losing sight of who I was. The caring, loving person I was began to turn into a frustrated and lost individual. This was when my inner and spiritual crisis took me on a path of seeking answers and healing.

Stopping and questioning our lives with 'WHY' our lives aren't making us as happy as we want to be is the beginning of your journey to finding the answers you're looking for. The answer that came to me was I was capable of making everyone around me happy except myself. I was acting for everyone else's happiness except my own. It was in asking myself the question 'WHY' that my answers flooded in. The child in me awoke, and my story began to unfold. It began when I had insights into what I was dealing with when my first memory came to me, and my bedroom image came to mind. Childhood sexual abuse was not part of my understanding at the time. As children, we were told to be aware of strangers who could hurt us, not that it could be a family member. So, the world of a family member hurting me was a world that was new to me, a world that lay dormant inside of me for many years. A world that I had held suppressed for far too long. A painful world that now had a gateway opened, and memories of what happened to me from the past came flooding in around my relationships with my parents and my outer family. At this time, I learnt that my inner world was creating my external experiences.

As children, we can only process what makes sense to us. Anything outside of the parameter of our understanding gets suppressed or locked away. This is what happens when we are abused as children. As a child, I was experiencing sexual abuse outside of my comprehension, and it was hard for me to process it. My distress was recognised as looking for attention, being stubborn, making up stories, lying, or just being plain naughty. There was no support from outside of me that recognised something was wrong and that my behaviour as a child was me crying out for the help I needed. Without that kind of support, I could not process what was happening to me or help make sense of it. So I shut it away. I recognise now that within my relationship with my husband and other men, I was creating the abuse for myself from the patterns I had learnt as a child trying to survive the abuse. As an adult, when the memories came flooding in, I felt that I was holding an unhealed part of myself and needed to find the support I needed to make sense of it and bring understanding and healing to what I was remembering. The child in me went to sleep and shut down her inner being to be able to live within her external world. She disappeared, and only those around her became her visible compass throughout her childhood. This became a pattern for my adult life as well. I was unable to listen to myself fully or to voice how I felt, and so my internal compass would become overwhelmed and confused in my relationships around love. I had no real idea of what was loving in my relationships, where I felt safe, and where within my everyday life I was functioning in a way that was loving towards myself and others too.

Every healing begins with a first step. My first step was calling the Rape Crisis Centre and finding a therapist to support me. At the time, I had no idea how to find a therapist as I had never been to a therapist before and didn't know anything about the kind of support I needed. For those looking to find a therapist, I suggest you research the kind of therapist and therapy you may need based on what it is you are dealing with. When it comes to childhood sexual abuse, look for a therapist who is trained and skilled in dealing with childhood trauma or just trauma.

I have experience both as a client going into therapy and as a therapist dealing with a person coming to therapy. My journey has given me many insights not only into my own experiences but that of others as well. The one component I feel we are all looking for is to be seen, heard, and have our feelings acknowledged. As a child from the '50s growing up, the phrase 'children should be seen and not heard was constantly said around me in my childhood home, and also, it was my father who dictated the rules in our home. Dinner would be on the table at a certain time each day. As children, we would have to come in to say the rosary at six o'clock each evening (this was part of my Catholic upbringing), and my father would call us in before this time by whistling for us to come home. No matter what any of us children were doing, everything was dropped to say the rosary at six each evening, and we would all have to take a turn saying the decades of the rosary. This was very much a Catholic thing. The saying that the family that prays together stays together was emphasised over and over. I realised I prayed a lot in those days for the help I gave myself later in life.

As a mother and grandmother, I have learned much about dealing with a distressed child. When I first began to remember the sexual abuse in my childhood, I had no way of dealing with the inner distress I was feeling at the time. My sleeping child had awakened, and the pain from that awakening tore me apart. I was an adult dealing with inner distress, and that inner distress was the memories of being a child and the abuse that the child had undergone. The title given to how the memories surfaced is called having flashbacks. Having flashbacks makes it feel like the memories are real and that they are happening right there and then. Time and reason find another dimension to the reality of experiencing the now. Everything becomes clouded in the past, and the present vanishes as the images and feelings come more to the fore, and the memories feel like your reality now. Outside events trigger flashbacks when they come, and until you learn what your triggers are, you have no way of gaining control over them.

My experience of having flashbacks and the emerging memories were telling a different story to the memory of my childhood that I had carried around for so long and was happening to me in ways that I couldn't comprehend. I was acting out of character. I was anxious and panicky about being in a relationship with my husband and others. The acting out was related to experiencing another side of my childhood that I had put away somewhere in my brain, and now it was like a Pandora's Box had opened, and it contained secrets yet to be told. There was no way that the lid would shut again. The therapy I had entered helped me make sense of what these memories were telling me. There were times I felt I was losing my mind and later came to realise that I was reclaiming more of myself and becoming whole again.

I was becoming aware that the patterns in my relationships around love came out of the fear, confusion, and overwhelming feelings I had carried from my childhood and had somehow normalised them to be the way life was. Instead, recognizing how I was reacting at times was normal for someone who had suffered trauma in her childhood and was not a normal response to a healthy way of being in relationships. It all began with recognising that there was something off with how I was dealing with my relationships.

Even though that recognition was there, I still did not know what that 'off' piece was for me until I understood that I had childhood trauma within me.

Those first memories of being abused began in the Post Office that day in March and came at night when I was in bed. I would wake up in terror from my nightmares of being abused. Nightmares are the brain's way of processing experiences and filing them into your memory system. My body would shake, and the clear images of my childhood bedroom would emerge.

I would be so distressed by the memories that I would wake my husband up to relate to him what I was remembering. I was attending therapy at the time, trying to deal with and make sense of what was happening to me. I needed to understand why this was happening to me now and why it hadn't come up sooner.

Seven years had passed since my parents died, and I was in the process of remembering and getting to grips with what I was remembering. I am the eldest in my family, and I stepped into some of the roles they had when they died, especially my mum. I was married and had two young children, yet I cared for my siblings as my mother had done before she died. It wasn't something they asked me to do. It was something that I was trained to do because of the childhood abuse that I had suffered. This carried on, and then I took on being there for friends when they were in crisis. I now know it was a pattern I had learnt from childhood to fly from my pain of abuse and to look outside of myself to the pain others were in. I was using that pattern to escape my grief and suppress the memories I didn't want to deal with again. There were times in my adult life when I would have had memories of my bedroom as a child and hearing footsteps on the stairs. At these times, I could not connect with them and the meaning they had for me. I was experiencing these images more daily and beginning to make sense of their meaning. Only when I stepped into my feelings was I able to start connecting with the images and the messages they were giving me, which were always frightening. As I said, it felt like I was in a puzzle trying to put the pieces together. I would go about my daily routine, and suddenly, I would feel like I was living the memory right then and there. The memory became my reality, as if it was happening to me at that moment. I felt frightened and could not understand what was happening to me. At that stage, I didn't realise how long it would take to put the puzzle together to create a full image.

Chapter 12
More About Flashbacks

Flashbacks are frightening when they come. They transport you back to the time of the trauma and can exist as if the trauma is happening right then and there to you. All sense of time and space is lost as you are transported back to the trauma scenes. The images, the sensations in the body, and the feelings all come in a rush, and it is very hard to get a handle on what is happening. That's where therapy comes into being of support to enable you to ground the flashbacks and bring yourself back into the reality of now. It takes a lot of practice, but in the end, it is worth it to provide the skills needed to deal with the trauma of the abuse. It also helps you to understand that circumstances in your adult life add to the memories being triggered.

It was in understanding what flashbacks were that helped me get to grips with how to manage them. Flashbacks are memories. At the time they are happening, it seems like they are real. You have seen soldiers in movies that come back from a war and hear the backfire of a car, and it triggers them into the scene of being shot at in the war; they fall to the ground thinking that it is happening to them now. Flashbacks are triggered by sound, taste, smell, or feeling. Understanding what triggers the flashback is how I got a handle on how to cope and ease them. Identifying what triggered my memories helped me to be able to distinguish what was going on in my inner world and realise that my external world was not the same reality. I kept a journal of what triggered me, and with my therapist's help, I set a plan that helped me manage and ground myself in dealing with the flashbacks. Here are some suggestions that have been of help to me and may be of help to you in managing your flashbacks.

Managing flashbacks:

To manage flashbacks, you must remember that you can feel terrified while not in danger.

Flashbacks are powerful and intense internal experiences that do not reflect external reality.

The external environment may have triggered a flashback, such as smell, sound, or visual stimuli reminiscent of past experiences, but this does not mean you are in danger.

To truly assess the actual danger, you must monitor subjective internal sensations and objective external reality.

During flashbacks, you become over-focused on internal cues rather than actual reality. Your alarm system is already on a high alert default setting, so it fails to register whether the environment is hostile or safe.

REMEMBER: if you cannot evaluate true safety, you also cannot evaluate actual danger.

Internal dialogue can be statements like 'He is coming to get me. She is making me do things I don't like. When we talk like this within ourselves, we use the present tense, which gives more power to the flashbacks. When talking about flashbacks, we need to refer to them in the past tense, e.g., 'I was attacked, I had to do things I didn't like. These statements bring the flashback into the past tense.

Create an anchor for yourself. An anchor is something that you can focus on that is in the present moment. It can be an object from the present that you can look at, hold, feel, or smell (make sure it is a present-day smell that creates grounding for you now).

Look outside yourself, recognise external senses, and name them out loud, e.g., 'I can see the sun shining. I can hear the birds singing; I can smell coffee.'

Evaluate your surroundings by noticing the colours, shapes, objects, people, and sounds around you. When we can see our surroundings clearly, we can remind ourselves of where we are now, that this is just a memory, that it is not happening now, and that there is no danger.

Stamping our feet on the ground helps us to connect with where we are now.

Carrying a favourite stone that brings good memories is another tool to hold onto and squeeze tightly in your grasp. It is easy to carry and access when you need to create a firm hold on your reality when a flashback occurs.

Chapter 13
More Memories Arise
(Trigger Warning)

Within the first few days, then weeks and months that followed in my therapy, more memories came, and I could clearly understand what had happened to me as a child with the first family member and how it was dealt with. It was something that my parents knew about and pushed under the carpet. No one was told about what had happened to me, and it was never spoken about again. The child in me was so traumatised by what my abuser did to me. I had been woken from my sleep by him in a drunken state. His action of making me perform oral sex on him was one where I nearly suffocated with the force of his action; at another, he was touching my body, which responded with pleasure to how he touched me, and this left me in conflict with my mind and body for years around touch and pleasure. Adult sexuality is outside the realm of a child's understanding. Being touched inappropriately or asked to perform and partake in a sexual act with an adult is traumatic for a child. It affects how, as an adult in later life, being in a sexual relationship with another adult can trigger unknown feelings around being touched or asked to partake in adult sexual acts, which can reignite all the unresolved feelings that have been suppressed as that child. My own sexual relationship with my husband was affected by how I saw myself as a woman by the trauma of that event, and my response within a sexual relationship was to numb out if I felt uncomfortable with anything I was asked to do. Not being able to voice or understand what I was feeling from the unresolved trauma that lay deep within me. In ways, the memories were there; I had yet to associate those with being sexually abused as a child. It was with these memories I first entered therapy with. I can't even begin to describe the terror and anxiety I lived with as I processed these memories. The distress at being touched in my relationship with my husband and the flashbacks that came at the time of being touched by him. I reverted to being the child, not the adult woman I was. Those times were distressing for us both. The world of sexual abuse had never entered my mind until the door to my memories was opened, and what had happened to me was named. From the start, it was hard to comprehend the naivety of myself as an adult and the innocence of the child in me to what had happened to her.

As I progressed through therapy, I began to feel very uncomfortable about speaking about another member of my family. When this family member was around me, I noticed how I felt uneasy and that I regressed to feeling more like a child than the adult woman I was. I didn't like being left alone with him and couldn't make sense of these feelings. I felt that, at times, I was numbing myself around him. I didn't recognise this fully at the time; it was only when I began to talk about him in my therapy that I could identify how I felt when he was around my children and me.

The more I worked on my feelings in therapy, the more I felt that there was more to my story and childhood than I was admitting to myself. Again, the flashbacks began, and I was taken to a ritual that was ongoing at weekends; the feelings that accompanied these flashbacks and the fear I felt in my body were all telling me that there was more of my story to unfold. It took a while to conclude that my feelings around this family member were similar to those I had around the other members of my family.

Finally, I accepted that I had been abused by another family member, also. Again, with this acceptance came the flood of memories and the heartbreak of knowing how I had been treated by yet another member of my family. It brought me to a very dark place within myself. A place I thought I had no way back from. Depression overwhelmed me, yet I kept going daily to look after my children and keep a daily routine. It was my way of learning to control what was happening to me. I was soon able to control the flashback with the aid of my therapist and found other avenues that led to my healing. I went into training to learn more about healing, the energies in my body, how my mind influenced my emotions and actions, and to bring about the integration I needed to bring healing to my life and reclaim the lost parts of myself from childhood.

Our journey toward healing can begin in many ways. What was happening to me was the beginning of my healing and towards a journey of reclaiming the lost child in me. I had separated from parts of myself that I could not fully understand as a child, and now it was my journey to find the answers and the skills to help my child understand herself, her pain, and those around her and the impact all this had on her life, my life.

Healing starts with the first step we take, and for me, it was in going to therapy to deal with the flashbacks and to understand how the memories I had suppressed had impacted my life even though I had not fully remembered them. The reactions I would have in my relationships and my patterns of dealing with others stemmed from the past I had shelved somewhere inside of me, yet they leaked into my life and caused me so much pain. It was the pain and the lack of direction for this pain that was causing my life to be in turmoil. As I began to understand and learn more about how shock and trauma impacted me and my ability to be in my world, I understood that the shock and the trauma were the problems, not me. I had blamed myself for too many years for something I had no control over as a child and was given the responsibility by both abusers who had no control over their actions other than to blame a child for them.

I spent my life thinking that I was responsible for all that was happening in my life. This is something that I took on as a child because of the trauma of the abuse. A child cannot know that the adult is to blame, so they blame themselves instead. As an adult, I took on more responsibility for others than I needed to. I never once looked to another to blame for what was happening as an adult. Taking on responsibility became healing in my life as it helped me take charge of getting the help I needed and gain more understanding and knowledge of the impact of childhood sexual abuse. I realised that in having learnt to take responsibility for others, I was giving others in my life a place to put the blame on me and not hold the responsibility for themselves. Knowing my story seems to give others a reason to hang their behaviours towards me on what had happened to me as a child. I became a scapegoat for their problems. Now, another part of my journey began, from easing my internal distress to creating an external world that broke the pattern of the over-responsibility I took for others' lives.

Everything I say about my learning and experiences may or may not be something that will resonate with you. I hope I will give you food for thought, and as you hold this book in your hand, some of my life experience has drawn you to read what I have written. Healing is personal to each of us, and we will start our journey at the point where the need for healing is showing up in our lives today. It may take us back to other times, not to blame, but to understand and to help us move forward to a new beginning in some areas of our lives. I have talked about this book for many years, yet it has never found its way to this beginning. I know now this is the time to bring it to birth and to share with others what I have learnt in the hope that I can be of support to others on their journey and bring healing, inspiration, empowerment, and guidance towards the path you will step upon on your journey.

Chapter 14
Body Talk

Our bodies are the messengers of what is taking place in our minds and subconscious. When we dismiss our thoughts before asking if these are true, we resist what our thoughts are bringing to us and the value of these thoughts towards our healing.

The tension and pain I felt in my body signalled that I was ignoring what my body was telling me about myself, the situation I was in as a child, and how it was still impacting my life as an adult. Here's what happened to me just recently. Each morning, I woke up feeling anxious about my day ahead. I couldn't fully grasp where all this anxiety was coming from. In my questioning of the anxiety, I recognised it was something I had lived with from my childhood and was now triggered by what was happening around me.

We have come through some anxious times in the last few years regarding COVID-19. Any crisis that creates anxiety can trigger us into survival mode to help us overcome that anxiety. In the beginning, because of all the continuing cases, rules, and regulations, the anxiety that was there kicked many of us into survival mode because we felt we were not safe regarding the virus. Cases rose and fell, and yet the virus is still not leaving us, and we are living with whatever was activated for us at the beginning of the virus being announced and is still impacting everyone and their lives even as I write this now. We each had our anxiety about what the virus was triggering for us. For me, it was around the safety of my family and myself, as I am sure it was for others. I hadn't recognised that it was also triggering past anxieties in me. I had spent my childhood being anxious around my siblings in connection to my abusers; I was anxious about being left alone too, and somehow, what was happening in the world was triggering not only my anxiety in the present but also my anxiety from my past. I could feel it, and the reaction was tension and pain, upset stomach, and night sweats. When I finally stopped and accepted my anxiety in the present and stayed with it, I could tap into the anxiety I had been carrying since childhood. I began to be able to separate it from the anxiety I was experiencing at the present moment. I reassured the child within me that the anxiety I had felt as that child may have treads of past anxieties, yet they were different. In helping myself become aware of how I was, I could separate from the anxiety I experienced as a child and gain control of how I was with the anxiety in the present moment. By acknowledging the differences between the past and present, I could find the solutions to ease my anxiety. Our past experiences, if not acknowledged and accepted, carry into our future and create the same patterns. If we want our future to be different, we must recreate our experiences and know the impact that they have had on our lives. Listening to the tension or the pain in our bodies are the signs that give us direction to healing from our past and creating a different future for ourselves.

Louise L. Hay's book *'You Can Heal Your Life'* continues to offer me profound insight into the relationship between my mind and body. How my thoughts and experiences from my past create who I was at the time before I began to remember, and how I lived out my experiences as a child in my adult life before my memories emerged. When our lives are not working for us the way we would like them to work, we need to spend some time relating to how our thoughts create our feelings and, in turn, how they affect our bodies. If we think of a negative thought, we create a negative feeling and create tension or pain in our bodies. The energies from our thoughts, feelings, and actions interact with each other. Sometimes, either one of them can be more present at a time; for instance, our feelings can be more prevalent if this is our go-to for understanding, and our minds may be out of sync with our feelings. Our feelings (intuition) can be saying that something is off, and yet our mind can try to convince us that we are wrong. It is in the questioning of where the thoughts or resistance are coming from that we can learn that the voice within our minds is not our understanding but that of another's.

Chapter 15
Making Sense

FEAR DEFINITION – *an unpleasant emotion caused by the threat of danger, pain, or harm.*

There is another meaning attached to fear: **FALSE EVIDENCE APPEARING REAL**.

A lot of the time, as adults, we can perceive the threat of danger, pain, or harm from the experiences we have had in the past, which persons or events in our adult lives can trigger. By knowing how to tell the difference between then and now and that, we, as adults, can gain more control in our lives than we had as children.

As children, when we experience the threat of danger, pain, or harm, we have one of four responses. The first is to run or take flight; the second is to fight back, which is difficult for young children, especially if the aggressor is an adult. The third response is to freeze or to play dead. I am sure you have seen animals in the wilderness being chased by their predator, and when the predator catches up with them, they don't fight back but play dead. This has saved many an animal's life. After a while, you will see the predator get tired of playing with the animal and walk away, only to see the animal sometimes getting up and running away when it feels safe.

When a threat is severe for us as children, we freeze and leave our bodies until the threat is over. It leaves an imprint on our brains, and if it is constantly happening to us, our brains become wired to be alert to the constant danger. Even years later, our brains can still be in this state of alert and freeze if the threat hasn't been treated for us as children and the threat removed from us. Lastly is to go into a fawn state. Have you ever seen an animal in the dark and headlights come upon it, and it becomes dazed for a second before it moves?

This can sometimes happen to us before the action we need to take comes into play.

When the trauma and shock are healed in childhood, we are more likely to be able to deal with trauma and shock in adulthood. Whatever support was there for us, we can carry it through to adulthood and have the skills and a way of dealing with other traumas or shocks in our lives. When trauma or shock hasn't been dealt with when it has happened, the defence that kicks in to help us survive at that time stays in place, and if the event that has caused the trauma or shock continues, our brains become wired to be in that defensive mode to help us to keep surviving even long after the trauma shock and threat has stopped. In later life, someone or something can reignite the trauma, and we react as if the event is happening in our present lives. This is when we are triggered, and all the past fears arise and seem so real in the present moment. We can be transported back to a time in our lives when the threat was real, and we dealt with it by running, fighting, or freezing to safeguard ourselves. As children, we have no way of protecting ourselves against the adults in our lives, and our brains kick in to protect us in any way that keeps us safe in the moment of threat. It is, as adults who recognising there is an impact on us that doesn't relate to a present circumstance, that we heal and rewire our brains into feeling safe again.

When I experienced flashbacks, I felt like I was transported back in time, and it felt so real in the present moment. It was hard to realise what was real and what was memory because flashbacks are just memories. Memories buried so deep as a child rise to the surface to be healed. It can be hard to comprehend all of this at the time of having a flashback or memory before being able to deal with these in therapy. A therapist can help you gain the skills you need to help deal with the flashbacks and also to help you acknowledge what had happened to you in childhood.

When we talk about FALSE EVIDENCE APPEARING REAL, this is what a flashback is. Within my therapy, I began to learn to see what was in front of me, to learn who I felt safe with, why I felt safe and unsafe with someone, and to learn what I needed to help me heal from my childhood. It was a time of great confusion, and I was always trying to live a daily life as a wife and a mum.

No one knew the depth of my distress outside the therapy room. It was where I felt safe to explore what was going on for me and the emotions that were churning inside me. To say I was fearful at this time was an understatement. I realise now that I had lived with the fear and had ways of lessening it through how I coped with it as a child. So, some of the strategies I learned as a child were also helpful in how I dealt with my present reality as an adult.

Whatever strategies we learn as a child to protect ourselves are not always damaging but ones that enable us to survive and get on with our daily lives. Only when some of those strategies cause us pain in our adult lives do we search for the healing we need as that child. My breakdown, or breakthrough, as I call it, was the awakening I needed to heal my past and help the child in me become whole again.

Know that healing is possible if you see yourself in anything I have spoken about right now. It may take time, and it will take as much time as is necessary. I started by going to therapy, which brought me on a path I hadn't gotten off. It has brought me many wonderful people who came into my life when I needed them; also new learning and new knowledge, skills that both help me and others, made me a more insightful parent and grandparent and has brought enhancement and deep understanding to my relationship with my husband and other men in my life.

So, what is my message to you as my reader? If anything is resonating with you as you read, know that healing is possible from childhood trauma, and physical, mental, emotional, and spiritual abuse. It all begins with you and your desire for your healing. You may begin like I did, wanting to know how I had lived a life, not remembering what had happened to me in childhood and making sense of all the emotions I was feeling and what messages my body was telling me about the truth of what had happened to me. You may remember and still have nightmares about what happened to you and not know how to ease the pain of the memories you have. You may be dealing with an ocean of emotions overwhelming you now; you don't know how to deal with them. You need to know that all these experiences can be healed, and you can find happiness, joy, and love. I am not saying it will be easy at times. I am saying that it will be worthwhile and that there is light at the end of the dark tunnel you may be in. I am here to help guide you towards your healing by sharing what I have found works for me in the hope that some of it will also benefit you.

Today is yesterday's future, and tomorrow is today's future. By taking a step each day towards your healing, you are creating the future you envisage for yourself. Within a year, taking a small step each day, we are closer to creating the future we want. The first task is to have a vision of what you want differently from your present moment. Imagine yourself standing in this future and how you will look, feel, and be. Come back to where you are today, and what would you want to prioritise in your life? Write down five things you would like to change about where you are within yourself. It's an inner journey you take before you create an outer one. It is in knowing yourself and developing within yourself better-coping skills, better reactions to your life, and knowing what you need to grow into yourself more and then create the life you dream for yourself.

My dream was to feel more connected to those I loved. The first place I had to start with was more connection with myself. Having a loving relationship with myself and understanding how that relationship was damaged in childhood by the message I got from others about myself. As children, we can be given a load of darkness from those around us when they have no idea who they are. I was given that from both my parents, and it is not to blame them as they received their darkness from their parents and the society they lived and grew up in. Every one of us is affected by darkness to one degree or another. We know this when we feel we are acting out in ways that we feel uncomfortable with and that we know can be harmful or hurtful towards ourselves or another.

I knew that some of my behaviours as an adult in my relationships with men especially were not how I wanted to behave, yet they seemed so much out of my control. I came to realise that they were out of my control as a child; I just hadn't realised that they were in my control now as an adult. When I grasped this, my life took a turn for the better. I created new boundaries for myself that helped me feel safe. In doing so, I got to know those around me, which also gave me the feeling of being safe in their company. It is within your power to change your life; you must take the first step. The first step is knowing what you would like to change for yourself right now, looking for the guidance you need to take the first step, and finding whatever or whoever is of support to you in taking the first step towards other steps that you will need in your life. It might start with sharing with a friend where you are and how you feel. We create more pain when we hold things inside and stay silent on how bad things are for us. When we share who we are with others, we begin to grow, especially if the person we share holds what we say with respect and love.

Chapter 16
Speaking and Remembering Emotions
(Trigger Warning)

As a child coming from being sexually abused and not having the comprehension to speak about it, I would find myself staying quiet in my relationships. I couldn't identify what I was feeling and how the behaviour of another at times upset me. Silence is what holds any abuse in place. Finding ways of expressing ourselves is important to break the chain of abuse. How do we do that? It took some time within my therapy to come to terms with and understand what I was feeling and how the memories matched my feelings. When feelings are denied as children, we also deny the child's intuitive parts. Knowing something doesn't feel right and having this dismissed as children, we learn to dismiss these feelings for ourselves. A child coming into a room, seeing its mother crying, for example, and asking what is wrong, having the mother deny that there is anything wrong confuses the child. The internal knowledge of the child is shut down as its external world does not match the feeling of knowing that their mother is upset. The mother denying her upset gives the child the message that what he is feeling and seeing isn't real. Confusion arises, and the child becomes unsure of himself. Whereas if the mother had acknowledged that she was upset, the child could learn to trust not only what it is feeling but also what it is seeing. The mother can reassure the child that there is nothing for it to be concerned about as the parent has it under control, even if it is upsetting, giving the child an even deeper understanding that even though things may be upsetting, they can be sorted out. This adds to the child's trust in himself and the confidence to know that they, too, can overcome upsetting things.

We deny our ability to trust ourselves and our healing by denying our feelings. In the beginning, I found it hard to express what I was feeling or even fully understand what I was feeling. I tried, at first, to express myself, and usually, I wouldn't be able to get across the full meaning of what I was expressing due to my lack of understanding of what I was feeling. I would try to express what I was feeling in the hope of getting understanding from others who were also struggling to understand what I was saying to them. Instead of creating the close relationships I wanted, I seemed to be disconnecting more from others and myself. The only way I could gain an understanding of myself was by speaking out about what I felt with my therapist. Together, we created the clarity I needed to express what I truly wanted to say. It is hard to make yourself heard when you are confused about your feelings. Taking the time to clarify what you are feeling is important for your understanding first and grounding it and then having the clarity to express to others those feelings with confidence.

When you are not used to expressing your feelings or emotions, they can initially feel quite intense, even scary. I knew I didn't want to blame another for hurting me; I just wanted to let them know that they had hurt me, and I didn't know how to do that. I learnt to identify what I was feeling and how the other person was behaving that would contribute to how I felt and then to express it from a place of the feeling I had because of how they had behaved towards me.

If, like me, you were a child who was brought up without having their emotions or feelings acknowledged or only having certain feelings accepted and others rejected, then you too would have learnt to be uncomfortable with expressing your feelings.

Anger was an emotion and feeling that was denied to me. The memory of how my anger was dealt with by one of my abusers left me afraid to express my anger throughout my childhood and adult life. As a young child of around two years old, I was asked to tidy up the toys I had played with. It was late. I was tired . I tried to help but somehow felt too tired to complete the tidying up and had a tantrum as a two-year-old did and refused to tidy up anymore. I was sent to bed, and my abuser accompanied me up the stairs. I was crying. What happened next took me totally by surprise. My abuser was so angry with me, threw me on my bed in a fit of anger and held my face down on my bed; I could feel something happening to my lower body that I couldn't comprehend, and the weight of his body against mine pushing my body and my face into the pillow below me. The pain was excruciating, and I thought I was going to die. I felt myself leaving my body. I passed out and felt that I was leaving my body for good. From somewhere, I could feel my body being shaken and asked what had happened to get me into this state. I do not recall when or how another person became present in the room with us. It was the distress of the other person and that person's call that pulled me back into my numb body. After that, I felt that I wasn't fully present in my body and didn't feel fully connected to my body for years. I know that it must seem inconceivable that something like this could happen to a child of that age and that there would be a memory of it. The pain I felt then would return consistently when I started my periods. I would feel a shooting pain in my buttocks enough to make me pass out. It was only through my therapy and dealing with the pain of what had happened as a child that I healed this pain each month. My symptoms began to disappear, and I could have my period without pain. In connecting with the memory and the feelings that memory brought to my body, I was able to heal the split that the incident had caused with my abuser at that time. By allowing myself to express the distress it had caused me at the time, I was acknowledging myself and the pain that had gone unnoticed by that incident. In this way, I was building a bridge through the trauma and, in turn, healing my body, and it all together solidified that this incident had taken place and that what I was remembering was real. I remember hearing my abuser say that I had done it to myself. That I had worked myself up into the state I was in was his explanation to the other person why I was the way I was when they entered the room. This began the process of taking on responsibility for all that would happen to me later.

Our bodies hold memories that sometimes our minds have split from. It is in making the connection to what we are feeling or thinking, exploring them as a whole, we make the connection and start to heal the pain caused by the trauma and shock we have suffered. At the time of the incident, when I was two years old, my mind and my body had split from each other. No comprehension brought them back together until I began to remember the abuse that had happened to me at that time. My abuser had used his body and his anger to assert his power over me. I don't know what the other person had made of what had happened because I cannot remember what had brought them into the room.

I found anger hard to express, even against my abuser in my therapy session. It would take me some time to get to the rage I had held inside me. The rage was more against me. I was the one who shouldn't have gotten angry. It was because of me my abuser did what he did to me. This was a pattern that I carried within all my relationships. Never be angry at the hurt others caused me. I was angrier with myself because it was something that I had done to create their anger at me. I constantly blamed myself. It also gave me the pattern of being invisible to my pain and seeing others' pain more than I did my own. I can look back now and see that I was a shadow of myself after that incident with my abuser and didn't reclaim that part of myself until I began to remember the sexual abuse in my later years.

I constantly suppressed my anger. I pushed it deep within me for fear of allowing it to surface and being punished again. I did this throughout my life, even into adulthood. When I did get angry, I would be distraught with how I had expressed my anger or would be in tears because I was unable or fearful of expressing what I was feeling and the anger I held inside. When a male expressed anger around me as an adult woman, I would cringe within myself, triggered back to that time as a child. I didn't realise this until some years later. Being angry is normal, especially when we are being hurt. It is a way of letting us know we want freedom from whatever happens to us, or it is a cry for the love we need. My abuser's anger was one of control and power over me as a child. He wanted me to do what he told me to do. Tidy up, and when I didn't follow through, his anger was my punishment.

What are you comfortable feeling, and what are you uncomfortable feeling?

How our feelings were accepted as children is how we will accept them now in our adult lives. Feelings are meant to be expressed. When we don't express them, they become like a pressure cooker with the lid on tightly, ready to explode. Unexpressed feelings manifest in our bodies through different sensations or illnesses. When we don't express our feelings, they land in our bodies as headaches, stomach aches, high blood pressure, and other similar symptoms.

It helps when we can identify our feelings. In doing so, we can acknowledge the feeling and look for how the feeling came about and why we feel that way. Our thoughts are what add to how we are feeling. How we perceive and think about ourselves is how we feel and act out. As children, we can listen to others' versions of who we should be or how we should act. When we don't meet the expectations of others, we then get a negative response for not living up to those expectations. We can be called names, e.g., like you are stupid, we can be put down as not being good enough, and as children, we are like sponges taking in all that is said to us, and these scripts become our self-talk to ourselves. We must catch how we talk to ourselves and the mind-set we have around ourselves.

Chapter 17
Mind-set

What we think is how we feel and how we behave.

We have over 60,000 thoughts on any given day. These thoughts are automatic until we become conscious of what we are thinking. Have you ever started your day out feeling good, and somewhere along the day, you find yourself in a negative spiral and wonder how you have gotten there? It can be because of our environment, listening to others' opinions, beliefs, and negative talk, or it can be that we lose track of our thoughts and pick up on others without even realising it.

If I asked you to name five positive things about yourself, could you do it easily? I can tell you from my experience with my clients and in the groups that I have worked with most people can tell you more about the negative feelings they have towards themselves than the positive ones. When you think negatively about yourself, you automatically make yourself feel not so good, and in turn, you can pull your energy down and act in not-so-positive ways.

To grasp what you are thinking, you must first ask yourself, 'Is it true?' what you are thinking about yourself. You can carry a pre-set programme within you that has nothing to do with what you think about yourself but what others have taught you to think about yourself. The environment you grew up in has given you messages about who you are and how you should be in this world. There may come a time when you decide, just like I did, that it is not who you want to be or believe yourself to be.

This is where the journey towards creating a positive mindset starts that will work for you and bring more of who you are to the fore. The first step is to find out what you are grateful for in your life right now. By doing so, you are acknowledging what is working for you right now and recognising the supports you have around you that are aiding you in creating more of who you are from your knowledge.

A child constantly being told that they are not 'good enough, 'not smart enough, or not enough of anything begins to believe that this is true of them. The only mirror they have that reflects that back to them is the mirror of the caregiver in front of them, and when they are constantly told they are not good enough, it becomes a belief they will carry forward into their adult lives. It becomes, at times, your self-talk. Have you been told that you are not good enough at any time? Is it something that you still believe is true for yourself today?

Challenging what you have been told about yourself is one of the mind-set changes you can make. Is there proof that you are not good enough at whatever you believe about yourself? Or is it something you avoid because of what you were told about yourself as a child that would stop you from even trying to do it now? Pick something that you feel you are not good enough to do. Question: who said this to you? Whose voice do you hear saying these words? Is it your voice or someone else's voice you hear? Ask yourself, is it true? When I have done this exercise with others, it is usually a parent's voice, a caregiver's voice, or a teacher's voice, or it can come from a religious person. When you question it, you find there is no truth to what you have been led to believe about yourself for years.

I constantly thought of myself as a bad person from the time I was a child into my adult life. I carried this belief within me based on my parents' opinions, mostly from my abuser. It was only in later years that I learnt it wasn't me doing something bad but my abusers. I firmly believe that most people are good; their behaviour at times is the thing that can be at fault, and that comes from how in their minds they think about themselves and how they have been trained to be by those around them. A lot of the time, this behaviour is there to suit the other person's behaviour and cover up for the wrongdoing they have done by blaming it on someone else; this is especially true in the abuse of a child by an adult as it was in my case as a child. The abuse I received at both my abuser's hands was never about their actions; it was more about how my being created these actions in them. So, I became the target of blame, and I believed that I was to blame for the abuse. That belief also leaked out into other areas of my life where I took on the blame for others' actions when, at times, it wasn't my fault.

So, getting our mindset conscious is important. Knowing how you think about yourself, especially negatively, will not make you feel good or act positively toward yourself. Can you change it? Yes. I am not saying it will happen overnight; it is something that you will need to work on constantly and consistently until you have reprogrammed your mind to think better of yourself.

Sharon Lowe, in her book *'The Mind Makeover,'* uses the image of a computer to help build a better mind-set. It is a book I recommend to help you gain better insight into how your mind can affect yourself and your everyday life. When we enter something on our computer that we want to keep, we save it. So, saving good things you think about yourself is one of the ways to build a good mind-set. When we are with others, and their negativity is getting to us, imagine yourself muting what they are saying, just like you would mute something on the computer or television that you are not interested in hearing. These are some of Sharon's suggestions to bring about the mind makeover she writes about.

Your mind is a powerful tool. It can be made to work against you or for you. That is down to you and your way of thinking about yourself. I have learnt to question what others believe about me and what I believe about myself. Can there be truth in what others think about me? At times, yes. I can acknowledge these times and change how I deal with their truth and my own. If it is the truth about me, I can question it and acknowledge it if my truth matches theirs; if not, it teaches me to believe in myself more. Your truth is something that you will discover for yourself. Listening to the messages that you are giving to yourself around yourself and how they make you feel will help you reprogram your mind to only think about what is the truth about yourself.

When you build your mind to focus on the good in you, you will become more aware of the truth of who you are. It will help you have more self-confidence, self-esteem, and self-belief in all of yourself and all you can do and achieve in your life. I promise this to you.

Chapter 18
Boundaries

Boundaries are something I have learnt to put into place for myself. Doing so has created more loving, healthy, and strong relationships. When we put effective boundaries into place, we keep our relationship with others strong and healthy. When we clearly communicate what our boundaries are with others, those around us know what our expectations of them are. In communicating our boundaries, we must know what we can tolerate and not tolerate from others. It is learning about our beliefs, our standards for our life, our opinions of things that matter to us, and having self-worth and good self-esteem.

When we are uncomfortable about something, and we don't speak up and communicate, our feelings of resentment can build up, and over time, this not only sends out the message that we can tolerate things that we can't, which leads others to continue their behaviours towards us. This is the time, then, to put into place boundaries for ourselves. Here are some insights into the boundaries you can put into place to help you feel more at ease and relaxed.

Physical boundaries refer to your body, privacy, and personal space. You may enjoy public displays of affection, or you may find yourself uncomfortable with this; you need to let others know. Sharing your preferences and expectations might feel difficult, especially if someone puts down what you are saying. Setting these boundaries is around you being respected for what it is you like, holds your self-respect in place, and gives the other person the knowledge that this is something that is important to you and that you want them to respect you.

Sharing your boundaries can improve your relationship with others. Knowing what you are and are not comfortable with and setting a boundary around them, e.g., if you need some time to relax after work and socialize, set a boundary around this. Doing this gives you time to breathe and honour your own needs. To have a consequence for not being given the space, maybe put it like this: 'I need 15 minutes to relax after work before we invite anyone over. If you invite others before I've relaxed, I will relax in private, and you will need to entertain them until I come down.'

Emotional boundaries are set when we are in touch with our own emotions. You need to know where you end, and others begin. If you are in a conversation where both parties are upset, you may need to create a boundary around this. Noticing when you feel guilty, ashamed, upset, and undervalued is of value in helping you put boundaries around the issues or situations that add to these feelings.

When we feel upset, and someone tries to fix it for us, we could feel that we are being heard or that the other person isn't listening to us, and this could lead to us feeling more upset than before. This is a time for a boundary to be put in place, e.g., When I'm upset, I would like you to listen to me without trying to fix it. I need to vent sometimes. When you try and fix things, I don't feel heard. If I want your advice, I will let you know.

Sexual boundaries refer to your expectations around physical intimacy. Again, knowing what is and isn't okay with you around frequency, sexual comments, and unwanted sexual touch. Expectations about others involved in your sex life and what sexual acts are preferred and off-limits should be communicated and discussed. Healthy sexual boundaries include mutual agreement, consent, and understanding of each other's sexual limits and desires.

Being sexually abused in the past can trigger the abuse during the sexual act in certain positions, and boundaries need to be set around that. You may also consider not having sex for a period, especially if you are only beginning to process your past abuse. Establishing boundaries around what is comfortable for you can help keep your sex life healthy and happy. You could say, 'I have a hard time enjoying a certain sexual position because it reminds me of a difficult experience. For me to enjoy sex, I need to avoid that position. I will let you know if I become bothered so we can switch positions.

Intellectual boundaries encompass ideas and beliefs. As we can have different ideas and beliefs, boundaries around respecting different views and ideas can keep your feelings from being hurt. When we talk down to someone, or someone talks down to us, treating us like we are not smart enough to understand or know what they are talking about can damage your emotional intimacy with yourself and with others. If you feel that you can't discuss certain topics with those around you because you believe that they don't respect your opinions or put you down, you need to put a boundary in place.

Being unable to share our views and opinions with others because of how others will react leaves us feeling hurt and upset. When you don't feel valued for your thoughts and beliefs, you need to communicate with the other person, especially if you want to continue being in the relationship with them. You could say, 'It hurts me when we disagree politically, and you tell me my opinion is wrong. It makes me feel like you don't respect my views. If you say my opinion is wrong, I will remind you not to and end the discussion if you continue to say it.'

Financial boundaries are around money. This is so important when we are in a relationship with another. Knowing what you earn and how that will be managed is important. Setting boundaries around how the finance is allocated helps bring more security to both parties. Things like joint and separate accounts, how much goes towards savings, what purchases you want to make, and how discretionary funds you will each have can keep you both on the same page where your finances are concerned. We all come from different backgrounds in what we learnt about money. We may have different rules and agendas for how and where we spend it, which can strain a relationship. Boundaries help to take that strain away when we put them into place.

Having open and honest discussions around your financial goals can keep your finances from becoming a point of contention. If you agree to put money into a separate fund to pay for a vacation and you feel your partner isn't contributing, this could upset you. You might say, ' I want to go on a nice vacation with you, but we both need to contribute to the vacation fund for that to happen. If you tell me when you contribute to the fund and how much you put in, I will match it.'

Boundaries help you function effectively, whether for yourself or within a relationship. Noticing when you feel disrespected, taken advantage of, or hurt is the time to put some boundaries that will help improve this for you. Knowing and respecting your limits and needs can improve how you relate to yourself and want others to relate to you, too. Boundaries are a way of keeping our relationship with ourselves and others healthy and strong.

For children who have been abused, their boundaries can be non-existent within their adult lives. So it is important as you heal your past that you learn to put into place the boundaries you need that give you back your space to feel safe, heard, and respected. Expressing your needs may not be something you are used to doing, and it may take some time to activate and set the boundaries you need for yourself. Boundaries are something that you can hold too tightly or too loosely. It is only in putting them into place that you learn how to hold the boundaries that allow you to open up your world to more safety, peace, and love for yourself.

Chapter 19
The Meaning of Love

Love is an intense feeling of deep affection. The art of caring and giving to someone else and having someone's best interest and well-being as a priority in your life. To truly love is a very selfless act. Love is patient and kind; love is not envious or boastful or arrogant or rude. It does not insist on its way; it is not irritable or resentful; it does not rejoice in wrongdoing but in the truth... Love never ends.

Of all these definitions of love and there is one thing I have learnt is that love has many meanings for us based on how love was missing in our lives.

As a child and an adult, I craved love, like most of us. I would bend over backward to gain approval and make others proud of me. This was the way I learnt to get and earn love from another. I had no real understanding of what love was other than what my parents and other caregivers in my life told me. I followed what I was guided to do to be loved, yet in later life, I became unhappy and felt unloved by continuing to follow the guidelines I had learnt as a child.

Love in my home was that what is said or done in our home stays in our home and is held within the four walls of our house. It was no one else's business what went on in our home. Where this sentiment can be of value at times for me as a child, it only served to hold the silence and secret that was the abuse and having no way of bringing it to the fore outside of our home.

Being told that we are doing it for your good was not the best reasoning for me as a child; even being told that we are doing it because we love you only caused distress and confusion in me. There were so many different versions of what love was in my life; the only one I wanted to feel was warm, happy, content, and at ease. I wanted that warm feeling of knowing that I was loved, which at times would flicker in and be gone again as quickly as it had arrived.

It was a roller-coaster of emotions. When I bring myself to the times I was alone in my bedroom, a warm feeling comes over me. It may not resonate with you, but for me, it was the presence of a light being that sat with me in that room and gave me the feeling of love and safety. I wasn't afraid of the presence. I welcomed it. It's hard to describe the daily visits from this light being brought to me. My parents would hear me talking to this being and put the term imaginary friend on this presence. They thought my loneliness had brought this imaginary friend into my life and were totally off the mark. This being had travelled with me from birth.

When people talk about near-death experiences, they talk about a tunnel or a blazing light meeting light beings in this space. I know I had about two experiences in my life where I had been in the presence of these light beings. These experiences came about through my therapy when I did some rebirthing techniques. One was at my birth, where it was doubtful if either my mother or I would survive the birth as my mum had complications due to having toxaemia at the last stages of the birth and was very ill at the time of my birth. It was a race to save both of us with the knowledge that one of us may die in the process. This was something that was related to me over and over throughout my childhood because of the distress my father felt at the time of my birth. I carried the belief that

I shouldn't exist because of being told of my father's distress constantly.

It was during my birth that I did die, as did my mother, and I remember going back into my birth during a healing session and both my mother and myself being in this light. It was a feeling of pure bliss for me and being there for some time until I felt the pull come back into my body. My mum and I never got to talk about my birth before she died, so I never got to hear how it had been for her at that time. That feeling of bliss stayed with me every time I saw the light being in my room. It was something I wasn't afraid of; I welcomed it.

I was very intuitive as a child. I knew what others needed to help them feel loved and cared for. I felt that I was always ahead of others' situations and could see what they needed for healing before they did. I relate this to an ability I gained with what happened to me as a two-year-old child with my abuser. I experienced being taken again into the light when I felt myself dying of the excruciating pain of my abuser's actions and how it brought me into another realm where I was embraced by this light again. I left my body, and only the shaking from the other person that came into the room brought me back into it. I was limp in their arms even though I was back in my body. I felt my spirit had stayed in that other realm. With the shock of what had happened, my spirit and body split from each other, and my inability to speak or understand what had happened left me disconnected from the inside. The other person in the room, having only the input from my abuser, concluded that I had brought this on myself by my hysteria about being punished by my abuser. It seems nonsense that that was the understanding in it. I just knew that from then on, I carried the feeling that I was bad and troubled, and that is exactly what my abuser wanted the other person to think.

Love was a very confusing word as I grew up, yet in the presence of the light, I felt what I wanted to feel from my parents and others. There was a split in me, one where I walked on this planet and one where a part of me lived on another. My energy was blocked in my everyday life, and at night, alone in my bedroom, I felt an energy where I could travel further than my life at that time could take me. Some might call this daydreaming or fantasizing about escaping the abuse, and yes, I would agree to some extent. I have learnt so much about how the brain reacts to trauma and shock, and yes, my brain did that for me, yet there was more to what I was experiencing than I could name. Throughout my healing, I learnt more about spirituality and energy and how we are not separate from God, the universe, or whatever you want to call the divine, but that we are part of the divine, and the divine lives within us all. As a child, I thought that I was separate from it and that it lived outside of me and not within me.

To feel whole, I knew that I had to embrace what I knew and gain more understanding of how all of this was creating my journey and the paths that led me to my healing.

Some of this could be freaking you out right now. I may challenge your beliefs and bring up some questions you may need answers to. The only thing I can say is that we all have what works for us, and my beliefs have worked for me throughout my life. I was never afraid of the presence of the light in my life until I reached adulthood and began to speak about it to others, and their reactions to me shut down this part of me because I didn't want to be different or to be seen as a freak. I shut it down for many years until I couldn't keep it down anymore, and I started to come into contact with others who were having similar experiences. I started to open up to those I felt comfortable sharing my experiences with no judgment on what they were hearing from me.

Support is another form of love. When we have support on our journey, it makes it all the easier to start to heal from the abuse of others. When we feel listened to and heard without anyone trying to fix us or tell us who they think we should be or what we should do, we have the time and space to emerge as the true beings we are. When we feel warmth, empathy, and compassion from others, we know we are home. From childhood to adulthood, the light was with me and constantly taught me about the love I needed. In later life, this experience helped me to recognise it in others and what it felt like to be loved and accepted just the way I was.

I am hoping that I am helping you be the best version of yourself, to listen to your inner calling, to recognise the love in your life, and to know that the journey you are on or being taken on is leading you in the direction of having that love in your life.

Chapter 20
On Being a Woman

Growing up, I experienced how the males in my life held a more important role than the females. It seemed that the male had a better stance in life, a more recognised stance than the female. It came down to the work that they each did. More priority was given to what the male worked at and how he would provide for his family. It was always down to the male to be the earner for his family and the female to be the homemaker. Roles I now see as putting pressure on both males and females to be someone they may not have wanted to be. The nurturing of the female to be an earner for her family was a lower priority and was considered not as important as the role of a female encouraged to be the home creator and to be there for the children. It felt like the male was put on a higher level than the female as an earner and not as a nurturer of their family.

It was a message that was not only held within families but within society and sometimes cultures that we lived in. The church had a huge influence on the lives of men and women. The message towards women was that they were of less significance than the male. We had a male image representing God within the catholic religion I was raised in. Men could go to be priests and be ordained by the church, whereas women couldn't. It is still the same to this day.

A few years ago, I studied Spiritual Accompaniment. It is a position where someone can come and reflect on how they are concerning how they view their God and their practice of religion or their daily connection to the spiritual parts of themselves. For the first year of the training, I constantly felt angry at how I was raised in my religion and how that impacted me as a woman. I learnt that not everyone had the same vision of the God I was brought up with and that the version they had was one of a compassionate and loving God. Our vision of our God or the Universe can be one of fear or one of love.

When asked to reflect on my image of God, it came as God the Father with no image of God the Mother. I felt I was invisible to the religion I was raised in.

There was no image of God the woman. The fear and anxiety I had learnt about a punishing God came from my image of my father as the only authority in our home and from the delivery of sermons each Sunday at mass about a vengeful God. The punishment of abandonment and isolation would occur if I didn't follow what was being preached and disobeyed my father and mother.

As children, we were to honour our parents when we may not have felt honoured by them. Children had no place other than to be at their parent's beck and call. This was my experience growing up in my household. My father was overly religious, and his beliefs were ours. I remember discussing his beliefs with him, questioning him as a teenager, getting my opinions and beliefs shut down, and enforcing his opinions on me. All of this contributed to how I saw my place in the world as a woman. I started to believe that as a woman, I was the one to blame for how I was treated and that I was the lowest of the low whenever I made a mistake.

I carried this throughout most of my life. Taking on the responsibility for how men treated me. That they had no control over anything they did in their relationship with me, that I was the one who had to control how they felt and dealt with me. There is nothing about them taking responsibility for their actions toward me. It has taken me many years and lots of therapy and workshops to value who I am as a woman. To undo all the programming about who I should be as a woman and what I am responsible for, and to build my self-esteem and self-love for who I am.

Society and culture have a lot to answer regarding how women are seen and appreciated in their homes, work, and relationships. I teach women to value what makes them the people they are and to know that there is an image of God they represent on this earth, too. If you haven't read The *Dissident Daughter* by Sue Monk Kidd, it is a book I would highly recommend that you read to gain a deeper understanding of yourself as part of God and a woman. I know it helped me open more to my religion, the interpretation of the bible, and where I fit into the image of God.

Coming from a background of sexual abuse in childhood, my whole sense of who I was as a female was distorted for me. I had been used and abused by the men in my life as a child. The child in me was damaged, and the image I carried forward of myself as female was also. An image that portrayed me as an object of male pleasure. Of being powerless and having no control over what had happened to me, and how all of those related to how I saw the act of making love as distasteful and unclean, which then carried forward to how I was in relationships with men in adult life.

It is hard to return from this, but it can be done. Learning to love yourself as a woman is where you start and can bring up a lot of grief and pain. I know I was ashamed of how I had allowed myself to be treated in my adult relationships with men. I finally understood that the abuse in my childhood had primed me to treat myself like I did and to allow men to treat me in ways that lowered my self-esteem to one that sometimes felt like it was in the gutter. A lot of the time, it was all done in the name of love, and this is what my abusers had taught me about their abuse of me: that it was because they loved me, and if they didn't love me, they would not be reacting to me the way they did. It was a message about myself as being loved that always frightened me when I was older when I was told how much someone, especially men, loved me.

Building yourself up after abuse can be as difficult as learning to love yourself after years of that love being distorted. You can question who you are and if what you feel is real love or if it is something that you have been told to believe. Defining what love is for you is the most important part of your healing on this journey and what aspect of you needs healing the most. A lot of the time, our mental image of ourselves needs healing, and the understanding that what happened to us created a survival mode for us that we carry forward and have learnt to be what love is for us.

It was getting myself around what happened to me as a child, understanding how I had coped and how that impacted my life later. I wanted to understand why my abusers had done what they did, and I can only guess that somewhere in their backgrounds, they saw and were taught that what they were doing was love. The time they grew up in, the losses in their lives, what had happened to them as children, and how their lives spanned out after that, I am sure, is what led them to do to me what they did. It was also important for me to be believed and have that belief in myself. For me, this was a struggle for many years as no one in my family believed me or remembered any experiences of abuse by my abusers. That left me feeling even more hateful of being a woman as my abuse had gone on until I was around nine, and in that time, I was the only girl for eight of those years with my other siblings. I felt that because I was a female child, I was the one who got abused. I had a lot of rage inside of me because of this. Not that I wanted my siblings to be abused. It was just because I was a female, and it felt like it was only because I was female that I was abused. Being a female doesn't necessarily make you the only one to be abused. I have dealt with many men over the years. The abuse they suffered not only at the hands of men but also at the hands of women was so appalling that I sometimes wonder how a human being could hurt another human being like that.

There is healing from abuse. It used to annoy me when I watched a TV programme about an abused person and the message they would come across that they would never get over or heal from it. I can say that you can, with the help and support of those who have dedicated their lives to the research and understanding of the impact that abuse can have on all areas of a child's life and, in turn, teach them the skills to live productive and happy lives.

I hope what I have written gives you the hope you need right now. I hope that the insight into my own story will give you some insight into your own story and healing from it.

Chapter 21
Building Self-Confidence

Something I am constantly asked is how to build self-confidence within yourself. First, we need to understand that self-confidence comes from what we think about ourselves, how that makes us feel, and how we behave. Self-confidence can be built when we know what affects how we think about ourselves and how we feel about ourselves.

Self-confidence begins in childhood and how those in our environment taught us to be. If you were a child constantly put down, you would do the same to yourself. If you were a child encouraged and empowered to be themselves, you would have learnt to build confidence in who you are no matter what others outside of you think of you. Self-confidence is not fixed. It is something that we can learn.

As adults, we can be more in control of the environment that we live in most of the time. By environment, I mean the things we choose to watch on television, the people we have in our lives, and how we live daily. I have heard both women and men talk about their lack of self-confidence, and then when I hear what their environment is like and the people they have in their lives, it tells a lot about why their self-confidence and self-esteem are so low.

To build self-confidence is to have self-knowledge. Knowing your beliefs and opinions, strengths and weaknesses, and how you interact with others. External influences outside of yourself can keep you small and make you doubt yourself and your abilities to be part of something bigger. When we have dreams, there may be someone in your life who holds a realistic view of life, but when you share a dream with them, they keep putting you off, and after talking to them, you dim your light.

Living in a family where your ideas, opinions, and beliefs were dismissed or put down, you learn to dismiss your own opinions and beliefs. You then can carry what others have taught you to believe into your adult life and adult relationships. We give so much credence to what others think of us but not enough to what we think of ourselves. We can think we are stupid because we were constantly told this as a child. We grow up believing this about ourselves and don't challenge whether it is true. Every negative thing you were taught about yourself growing up has taken residency in your mind until you start to question what you believe about yourself. It can stop us from even trying out something new in our lives that we could gain more confidence in doing.

I have learned confidence when I challenge my fears of being stupid, not being intelligent enough, and not being good enough because I am constantly measuring myself against others. My mother would constantly compare me to other girls in our neighbourhood, within our families and friends. It knocked my confidence so much that I would try to do as well, if not better than others at first. I was being compared to them, which only dragged me down even more as I set myself against what might have been their strengths and not my own.

Knowing your strengths and weaknesses is important in building up your confidence. Take a sheet of paper or a notebook and write down five strengths you know you have. On the other side, write down five weaknesses that you have. If you come with fewer strengths and more weaknesses or vice versa, you have something to work with. Our strengths are the things we do very well, even automatically, as they have become second nature. Our weaknesses are those things we can work on to become our strengths and are usually the things we need to work on to create a better life for ourselves. When we can admit our strengths and weaknesses, we can feel more confident in our actions and who we are. For example, your partner says to you, 'You are no good with money,' and in knowing this, you say, 'I agree I have some problems with my finances, and I am working on correcting this; there is no more than your partner can say as you have owned what they said about you, you have acknowledged that it is something you know about yourself too and that you are willing to do something about it. The fact that you will do something about it will build confidence in your ability to take charge of something that was causing a problem not only with your finances but with your partner. It has a twofold conclusion. It builds up your confidence in managing your finances and more trust in your relationship around finance.

The internal voice within you also negates you as a person. I'm not good enough, not pretty enough; I'm too old, I will never amount to anything, etc. All this negative self-talk can stop you from trying something new and help you move forward. Again, many put-downs in our lives come from the put-downs we have experienced growing up, whether in childhood, our past relationships, those we are currently in, or societal influences of who we should be. This harsh voice inside us keeps us stuck in jobs we don't like and in toxic relationships and stops us from moving forward to what it is we would like to have in our lives. We know it is down to us to change, but how do we make that happen?

Questioning first the negative talk we give ourselves, who told us these things about ourselves, whose voice we hear in our minds, and challenging it with the voice that comes from within ourselves. Our fear of change can stop us from growing, and I know that it can be painful when we start to take care of ourselves and change our environment and those around us that hold us down. When we start to establish boundaries for ourselves and connect with like-minded people who help us grow more in our self-confidence, we are on a path to building up our self-esteem and our self-worth. Start by building on your strengths, get the support to help build up your weaknesses into being a stronger part of you, and set goals that are achievable and that, with support and small steps, can create the dream you want to build. Self-confidence is something we can build once we are willing to do so.

Chapter 22
Learning to Love Yourself After Abuse

So many times during my process and journey through remembering the sexual abuse in my childhood, I had to put myself first. This was a new concept for me as I was trained as a young child and girl to always put others before myself. The saying 'Love thy neighbour as thy self' got lost in translation to 'Love your neighbour before yourself' in my family. I watched as a young child how my mother would leave herself short of food by giving the largest portion to my father first and then portioning the food for us before portioning food out for herself. This was a constant practice in our home. It even lasted till the day my mother died. She had not been well all that week. She complained of pain in her left arm and had gone to the doctor twice that week, complaining of the pain to be told that it was arthritis. She called to see me the morning of her death, and we had tea together. She asked if anything should happen to her if I would look after my father and my siblings. I had no idea what this would mean for me at the time, and I agreed. My mum went home, cleaned her house from top to bottom, completed her ironing, and made dinner, a stew for the next day's dinner. She said to my father that she still wasn't feeling well and went to bed, where she died from a massive heart attack. Right till the end, she did everything for everyone else but herself.

Sometime later, I would look to myself for the care and love I needed to give myself. When my mum died, I took my mother's place and looked after my father and siblings. Looking back now, I can see I was in denial that my mother was not around anymore. By trying to fill her space, I wasn't giving myself the time to grieve and accept that she had passed and that I was left to look after my father and my siblings. Somewhere deep inside, what my mother had asked of me that morning of her death felt familiar from my childhood; I just hadn't yet put the pieces together.

My constant looking after others was bound to catch up with me at some point. A year and two months later, my father died in our home. About six months later, still in the role of carer, I was walking with my daughter and pushing my niece in her pram, and I felt tears roll down my face. I felt I wasn't going to be able to stop. I felt so distressed that I walked into my doctor and sat crying my eyes out, asking for help as I felt I couldn't go on anymore. He listened, prescribed some anti-depressions for me to take, and said he would make an appointment for me to see a psychiatrist.

I didn't take the tablets; I went to the psychiatrist for one appointment, and somewhere deep inside, I knew this was not the way forward for me. I pulled on a strength I don't know where it came from and made myself carry on as I was. I shut down what wanted to come out of me, even though I was not fully aware of what that was. Until I was ready to face what was trying to surface for me, I continued to carry on as I had before, and in doing so, I continued to stay in the same patterns I had brought from my childhood.

I realised that I constantly would keep doing whatever distracted me from what wanted to come up in me. I held onto the denial and resistance for some time. Again, I learnt that this was a way of coping I had learnt as a child. To put away the pain and to keep existing.

Time moved on, and it wasn't till nearly six years after my parents died that the memories came flooding in. This was the beginning of caring and loving myself more. I met with a lot of resistance to what I was saying about what I was remembering and the changes I needed to make in my life and my relationships. They say it is in times of crisis that you find out who your real friends are; that is what happened to me. I learnt that loving and caring for myself had a price. You need to be aware that in caring for yourself, after years of putting others first, things within your life and your relationships will change.

It is also hard to practice loving yourself when it has been ingrained in you to put others' care before your own. It is especially hard when you have children who need you to be there for them. I was the one in our relationship which they would come to with their problems. As I was sorting out problems in my past, I felt torn between their needs and my own needs and being a good mum at the time. I managed to do that even if it wasn't perfect at the time. My relationship with my husband was suffering at the same time. My husband found it hard to understand and sometimes to believe what I was saying had happened to me. I related to his lack of understanding as my lack of trying to make sense of what was happening to me. I look back now and see that I was accepting that this had happened to me in some ways, and in other ways, I was still unable to make sense of all of it. At times, I gave credit to what he thought about what was happening to me more because of my lack of understanding myself.

Loving and caring for yourself is something that you will only know how to do. You are the one who is in the process of remembering and the impact that will have on you and your healing.

How others perceive what you need is none of your business. What comes up for you and your needs will differ from those you would have had before because of the healing process you are in right now.

Loving and healing are personal to you and your journey. To heal, you need to change the beliefs you hold about yourself that others taught you to believe about yourself. There will be patterns of behaviours that you will change as these patterns don't serve you in the way they did before. They were patterns that protected you from the hurt and the pain that bought you the wrong kind of love. They will not serve you in loving and caring for yourself now as these require different behaviour. Loving and caring for yourself requires you to speak kindly to yourself, to have patience with yourself, and to show yourself the compassion that may not have existed in your childhood.

When you are so used to being harsh with yourself, criticising yourself, and feeling that you are a bad person and can't be loved for who you are, it takes time and as much time as needed to heal from all of this. There is no time limit on your healing. It will take as long as it takes. You will go at your own pace. Sometimes, you will move faster than others. The time it takes is based on the support you have around you in moving forward. I have learned that being supported is crucial to healing from any abusive relationship in your life. Being believed is another part of your healing as well.

For me, the start of my journey was helped by being listened to, acknowledging that something had happened to me, and believing that I was in this process of trying to understand and make more sense of all that I was dealing with. The Insights that came flooding in and when they matched the sensations I was having in my body as I spoke about them was something that firmly concreted for me and helped me believe in myself and my own story. My insights and my body were the beacons that lit my way through all that I was remembering. If you are in the same process, all I would ask of you is to trust whatever is coming up for you and explore it in a safe space where you are listening to your inner knowing and that all that you are remembering is coming from you. You are not being told what you remember from another.

Our journey through abuse and towards loving and caring for ourselves is one that we alone can make, along with the support of those who help us honour that journey and helps us make clear for ourselves that it is our story and we are not going mad or crazy.

Chapter 23
Restoring Your Trust in Yourself

Throughout your journey, before your healing began, you have often been in survival mode. As you process your memories, identify your feelings, and understand how you were made to feel and think about yourself throughout your abuse, you begin to emerge from the shock and the trauma with a better understanding of who you truly are. Now comes the process of trusting all that you have learnt about yourself in the past and the beginning of creating a new reality for yourself. How do you begin to do that?

The more you understand the effects childhood sexual abuse has had on you, the better you can prevent that kind of abuse within your own life as an adult. As I moved through the process of dealing with the abuse, I learned what my true feelings were at the time of the abuse. These helped me know the times I felt those feelings within my relationships in my present day. Once I had come out of the survival mode I was in at the beginning of my memories, I was better able to gauge my thoughts and feelings, not be influenced by others' expectations of me, and hold my expectations of myself for myself.

When we listen to our intuition or gut instinct, we can know when something is off for us. In feeling this, we begin to allow ourselves to trust these insights. Not to be forced into doing something we are not ready to do or feel uncomfortable with. To take the time out to fully grasp what sits right for us. It's okay to ask for time to reflect and consider what someone may be asking of you and also what you may be asking of yourself. I know when I had doubts about what someone was asking me of me, I needed time to reflect on it for myself. The doubts told me I needed that space to have a certainty that I could trust what I wanted to do and the clarity that this was right for me. If I felt forced to answer, I knew I was being disrespected, and my right to take time out and reflect was being dismissed. Our doubts are our inner signal that we are not sure about something. Taking the time to reflect on them by writing them down and working out how to gauge those doubts by how intense they are by using a scale of measurement of 1-10, one being so unsure and 10 having more clarity and certainty that this is the right thing or decision for you will help you judge your readiness to go forward with what is being asked of you.

The more I listened to myself, the more I knew my own beliefs and values for my own life. I began to build more inner wisdom within myself and, in turn, more confidence, self-esteem, and, best of all, more trust in myself and my needs. Being able to express my own needs, I began to focus more on them rather than always feeling the need to anticipate and respond to others' needs. As children, our way of survival is anticipating what others' needs are and meeting them to save ourselves from further harm and from the abuse we are experiencing. It was a way of protecting yourself and feeling you have some control over what is happening to you. In understanding your needs, you learn to know what feels right for you.

As you begin to trust yourself more, you develop more self-reliance, and the dependency on others lessens. At the beginning of my journey, I felt that I depended a lot on those around me to help me make sense of what I was going through. As I went further into my healing and knew how I felt and thought, I could rely more on myself to meet my needs. I knew when I needed help and support from others and when I could do things for myself. I know this is where my journaling came in, as I would record what was building my trust and what I needed to work on to gain more confidence within myself. This is something I would recommend you do, too. It helps you see how far you have come and helps keep you focused on holding onto all you have learnt that is helping you heal on your journey.

Coming to terms with my feelings around my childhood sexual abuse helped me be more in touch with my inner experiences, identify and express my true feelings within my relationships, and release the guilt and shame I carried from childhood into adulthood relationships. As I said earlier in this book, I struggled with how I felt because I was so out of touch with them, and they were ignored as a child. Feeling certain feelings felt dangerous for me, too, like my anger. So, I learnt to shut my feelings of anger down. When I began to allow myself to feel this anger, it frightened and overwhelmed me. I had to learn how to express my anger safely and assertively. I had to learn that there was a healthy way to express my anger and that it is a healthy emotion that helps to protect me from being hurt. I had to understand, too, when my anger was legitimate for myself. It helped me to write in my journal about my anger, express it to a friend or my therapist, or express it by punching pillows. When we lean into the anger and express it safely, we can reduce the anger or even rage we feel and learn to express it in a more grounded way by knowing that our anger is relevant to us. In expressing it, we give acknowledgment to the hurt we have suffered and decide how we want to express it and deal with it.

Chapter 24
Self-Care

As you begin to heal, it is important to know and keep up with your self-care routines. I begin my day with prayer, meditation, journaling, and reading some self-help books. This has been my morning practice for many years, and it works for me to begin my day on a positive note. When I don't get to do these, I can feel my day not being as positive or productive as I would like it to be. As you move forward on your journey, you must develop self-care practices that work for you and be consistent with following them through. You may find yourself going from being good with your self-care to avoiding it sometimes. It may feel like three steps forward and one back. It takes practise to hold onto new routines. You must know the benefits that come for you when you hold your self-care practices in place. The self-care practices I have put into place over the years have benefited me in progressing forward in building resilience, healing, and learning to have more empathy and self-compassion for myself.

As I progressed in my healing, there were times when I would have setbacks, and only through the self-care routines I had in place was I able to move forward from the setback with more ease and not allow myself to spiral down too far. I recognised that when I had a setback in my healing, it told me I needed more healing in that area. There will be challenges and setbacks; it's how we bounce back from them is important. I learnt that what would have set me back months with my self-care routine may only take a day or even a couple of hours to get back on track again. The more skills I had to manage my trauma and stress reactions, the faster I could ground myself and feel in control of my life again. All I learnt through my recovery helped me bounce back quicker than I would have at the beginning of my journey. As you go through your recovery and process, you will gain skills and understanding that will benefit you should you have a setback. Your self-care routine will sit comfortably with you. With the healing you have already done, you will never go back to the place you began in the same way because of the skills and awareness you have as you proceed through your recovery process.

Understanding what self-care is for you is knowing what you are comfortable doing and what you enjoy doing to uplift your spirit and bring positive outcomes into your day and life.

Chapter 25
Loving Relationships

Speaking about your abuse to others can isolate you from certain relationships, especially if it was a family member or members who abused you. I knew I had to evaluate my relationships with family, friends, and my husband when I remembered the childhood sexual abuse. To evaluate my relationships, I had to know who I felt comfortable around, who I felt safe with and could trust, who I felt listened to me, and how my feelings and needs were respected. Being able to express my needs was something I struggled with. I had to learn to be assertive, which took a lot of trust in myself. I had to learn what being assertive meant and how it is more positive than the manipulation, threat, and aggression used by my abusers to get what they wanted from me and know the differences between them. It is something that you also need to learn to create more loving and close relationships for yourself. Assertiveness is learning to have respect for yourself and others as well. It's not aggressively asking for your needs to be met. It is respect for the rights of others while holding respect for your rights in mind. Asking for your needs to be met doesn't always mean they will be met. It is expressing your needs to another in the hope that they can be met by negotiation with the other person.

In relationships, others may not want to accept what you are relating to them; you mustn't invalidate your feelings and needs. I know from my journey there were times I would invalidate my feelings in favour of others, which distressed me more. I felt at times I was stopped from expressing myself or I stopped expressing myself to hold onto a relationship. I would express myself in the hope of being heard, and because of the other person's reaction, I would close myself down. This was a familiar pattern for me that I learnt as a child. To break this pattern, I learnt that not with everyone could I be my true self, and that I had to let go of some of my relationships. It was hard at the time, but in the long run, it was the best thing for me to do for my healing and to hold the respect I needed for myself, my feelings, and my needs. I learnt that there were people I could be around and express how I felt with comfort and who respected my needs.

Chapter 26
Knowing Our Patterns

We hurt ourselves based on what we have experienced and been taught as children. This impacted me when I first realised what had happened in my past as a child was now my way of hurting myself as an adult. Until we begin to understand the patterns we carry not only from our families but from generations before us and also the environment we have been brought up in and the climate of the world at the time of not only our births but the births of the generations before us and how the imprints of all these create the person we are today.

I felt like crying for the number of times I had hurt myself as a woman because of what I had been taught to be as that female; what had been said and done to me became my way of being with myself. The more I blamed it on my parents or the abuse, I lost track of how I was doing the same things to myself. Until I centred myself fully on who I was, how I was, and what I felt, I could not change the patterns of my being. It wasn't until I recognised them for what had happened to me, the impacts they had on me on all levels of my being, and brought the abuse more into my reality I had no way of healing the child within me and the search for the love I craved. We all crave something in our lives, and that craving or longing comes from what we didn't have in our lives growing up and our dreams of how we long for our lives to be today. What we don't realise is that we have developed patterns of being that helped us get our needs met as children and still use those patterns in meeting our needs in our daily lives as adults.

In some cases, our needs were never met. The patterns we created then to get those needs met were patterns that probably got our needs met negatively rather than lovingly. In holding these patterns, we are recreating the same versions of what was there for us as children, and in doing so, we find that the happiness or love we needed is still not being met; we just learnt to adapt and create these patterns to meet our needs according to what others expected of us and not because they truly acknowledged who we are.

There is a screaming child within us all. Screaming for notice, screaming for love, screaming to be heard, screaming to be understood, and screaming to be loved for who we are. For a lot of us, these screams were put down and not heard, so we learnt not to hear our voices anymore or our screams and to hear from the outside of ourselves how others perceived us to be because of their projections onto us of how we should be according to who they thought we should be. We learnt to separate from ourselves, discard our true selves, and become what others said we were or wanted us to be.

Reclaiming ourselves is where we need to start, and usually, it shows up in our lives as adults when we begin to question and feel where our lives are taking us now. When we touch into the unhappiness of where we are. When we fret about not being good enough, not getting things right, or not having all that we would like in our lives and then begin to question what isn't working for us, this leads us to explore our world and the way it is right now. Not all the answers will come at a pace we want to take us out of the pain we are in, but at a pace that will help us make sense of our lives and bring about the changes we need to make.

When I asked the question 'WHY,' the answers flooded into me, and I became overwhelmed with all the information that came with that question. There was a conflict between the answers making sense and not believing what I remembered. Another world and another child in me came forward looking for the healing it had needed many years ago and didn't get, screaming from the now open wound to be taken care of and healed. I have learnt that what you long for in your life right now is the dream of the healing you need for your life, both past and present, and the discontent you feel is also telling you what is not working for you right now.

There will be questions you will have in your life that you are asking yourself right now, and looking for the answers you need to bring more love and healing into your life, ask the questions and listen for the answers; they are ready to unfold for you. Yes, it may be painful at times as you move on your journey, but there is light at the end of the tunnel. I can tell you now after my journey through remembering and creating the transformation I needed in my life and still to this day continue to make. It will take as long as it takes. As you walk through this process, the support you allow into your life will define that progress and how long it will be. Nothing is easy when change is involved.

Embracing my question of 'WHY' opened doors I had closed tightly shut from childhood. Yet, as I walked through the process of remembering, I could identify the patterns that existed in my daily life as ones I had learnt to gain the love that was the wrong kind of love for me. The concept of love I was taught as a child in my relationship with my abusers was the kind of love I brought to my adult relationships, and that caused me so much pain that I came to ask the question, 'WHY.' I needed to know the reason for my unhappiness and if there was something I could do or change about what I was feeling. It was a time when I felt I had hit rock bottom in my life.

The healing came and is a journey I have shared with you as my story unfolded through these pages. I have shared with you the tools that have helped me in the hope that some of what I share will also serve you.

The urge to write this book has never left me. I have backed away from it many times due to doubt about who would want to know my story and if it would be of any value to the lives of others. In overcoming my doubts and to be of service to others who may find themselves in the same or similar situations to myself at times in their lives, I decided to put my story down to be of service to you. You were drawn to this book for a reason, and I hope I can serve you as you read my story.

We all have doubts about being good enough, smart enough, brave enough, and many more. The only way to overcome these doubts is to do what you fear doing. So this is me right now, writing to you and telling my story in the hope that it will be of value to you.

Chapter 27
Coming to Terms with Ourselves

I felt the need to write this book to support those who have lived in an abusive environment or situation both in childhood and in their adult lives, to support them in their healing and creating more joy, love, and happiness in them and their lives, too. It comes from my heart to yours; it is in telling my own story and experiences that I might support you.

Traveling through any healing process, especially from childhood, can be as distressing as being abused. You are now connecting to a part of yourself that needed expression, support, and comfort at the time yet didn't get these needs met. It is the cry of the child to have those needs met now. You become the parent/caregiver to the child now, and because of the lack of experience from those around you or because of a cover-up of your abuse, you can have no way of knowing how to deal with this in a way that can bring the healing you need to yourself.

When I first began to remember my abuse, I felt I had a screaming child inside of me and had no way of dealing with her. I had no idea how to take care of the pain of remembering what had happened to me, and I knew I needed support to help myself get through it. The child in me I had held at a distance. It was like she was from another world, a world I hadn't remembered existed until after my parents died. That was the most painful thing at the beginning of my journey: I had no recognition of this part of me until I remembered it in my thirties. Even then, I found it hard to come to terms with the fact that I had been sexually abused as a young child. It felt beyond my comprehension as an adult, let alone as a child who had been through it.

Even though I said I was sexually abused as a child, it took quite some time before I fully grasped what I was saying was true. It was like a whole part of my life had been tucked away and belonged to someone else and not to me for years. Only after going through therapy could I see how the abuse played out in my life as an adult and in the relationships I had as that adult. Pieces of a puzzle coming together and creating a whole picture of my life.

This may be something you are experiencing in your life as you begin your journey towards coming to terms with your childhood sexual abuse and beginning healing from that abuse in your childhood. We all carry abuse from childhood to one degree or another; some are more devastating than others. I know that the abuse I suffered took from me the wholeness that I needed in my life. Every part of me felt fragmented and not integrated as a whole. Physically, mentally, emotionally, and spiritually, they were broken and not connected. I could function in some of these areas but not fully as I wanted to. I felt blocked in every way I turned; the block was always my own, running away from what I needed to heal. I lived only a portion of my life while the other was buried in a dungeon. The part that I held in prison began to scream to get out as it had had enough of how my life was going. As an adult, I asked why, and in doing so, I opened the prison door and let the demented child in me out by remembering how it truly had been for me at certain times and the scars that I carried that needed healing.

I have touched on how when we as children, especially very young children, can't cope with a traumatic event, our brains have a wonderful way of shutting that event off and putting it away so that we can feel safe and protected from the distress it has caused and especially when it has gone unnoticed by those around us. We have no way of making sense of it and have to store it until we can find a way to deal with it. When there is continuing trauma in our childhood, we can shut down that event and store it elsewhere. This is what happened to me. I am grateful for how our brains tell us when we are in danger, and we can run, fight, or freeze to protect ourselves, but as children, we have no way of fighting back or running, especially when it is an adult that is the instrument of the trauma, so we freeze. In the freezing, the trauma is frozen inside our brains, and it is only if it is recognised in us and dealt with it can begin to thaw the trauma experienced, and we can rewire our brains to connect more with what is safe for us now. When it isn't dealt with, it is kept in a deep freeze until we can take it out, maybe for many years from when the event happened.

Through my adult experiences, I recognized that something wasn't right in my life. It took some time to realise this, and I recognised it was in how I felt in my relationships, how I was dealing with my life, and how I felt about myself. I found it harder and harder to love myself within my relationships. I felt that I was the one who was the problem or caused the problems and that I would never be loved in the way I wanted to be loved.

It was a question of 'why' my life was like this and feeling that I was at fault that opened the door that let my child come forward and show me what had happened to her. As children, we have no words or comprehension of what has happened to us. As the adult meeting with my inner child, I could tell from myself the distress I was in within my adult life had a similar feeling to the child's torment in my childhood. Realising this, I could see the hurt and pain I was in within my relationships more. By connecting with my inner child, I could reconstruct how I wanted to be in my relationships. I wanted to be heard and listened to, to how I wanted my emotions taken into consideration, and to how I wanted to be loved in ways I hadn't before.

As I write this to you, I hope you can begin to understand some things for yourself and your journey. I remember speaking about what I was remembering to my husband and family and their reactions to what I was saying. The craziness I felt in myself at the start of my remembering was the craziness they treated me with. Their lack of understanding and my own made this so distressing for them and me and my children. The impact of how it was dealt with on my children saddens me the most. The fear and anxiety they witnessed in me confused and frightened them, and how those around me dealt with that added to their fears and upset. I had been the stable one in their lives more than others in our family. I was their constant in their daily lives, and now I was the crazy one, according to everyone around them and me at the time.

It's hard to look back at that time and see the lack of understanding, the judgments, the disbelief, and the put-downs of what I was saying as untrue. The courage and the distress caused by remembering and telling our stories is not something we do lightly. Why would I have wanted to put myself and my family through this if it wasn't true? It was something that I didn't back down on and became even stronger as I walked through therapy.

It takes time to walk through this journey, and I have learnt in dealing with others on their journeys through their childhood abuse to take their time to understand their process before revealing it to others. For me, it was a very frightening time, and it was something that overwhelmed me. It was finding a part of myself that I didn't know existed until the nightmares and the flashbacks that constantly awakened me to my reality as a child and as a woman and an adult. The sickening feeling I had about myself, how I was behaving in my relationships, and allowing others to treat me and cause me pain were all related to the abuse I received as a child.

I can recognise others now when trauma exists in their lives even before they have the recognition they need about it. I don't always know what that trauma is for them. Was it that they were not seen, heard, or felt at the time of whatever event they were speaking about? It shows how they react as they speak and how they feel. The pieces come together, and we can create a true picture for them. They have their knowledge, and I guide them through it.

If you are only starting your journey, I hope some of what I have said will aid you in continuing to walk on your path toward the understanding and healing you need. It is not an easy journey to take, but it is a worthwhile one towards creating the healing you want for your life. You will be guided to what is best for you when you listen to your heart and follow its guidance. When we ask to be healed, we are directed toward what that healing will be for us. You need to trust your instincts and intuition. To have faith, believe, and trust in oneself is a powerful way to become your true self, and I hope I have been of assistance in encouraging you on your journey towards reaching the goals you are setting for your healing. Take only what is relevant to you as you read my story.

Epilogue
Beginning Anew

With each step we take forward, we are stepping further from our past and moving more into our present day and our dreams for the future. We can't change the past; we can learn from it and, with that learning, create new beliefs and a new mindset for ourselves.

Back when I first started to remember the abuse I had suffered as a child, I was devastated at times, and at other times, I was relieved. These two conflicting emotions pull on me constantly, and the one I went to the most in the beginning was the devastating one. It felt wrong to feel sometimes satisfied by what I now understood about my relationships and myself. I had believed for so long that I was bad, not enough, not desirable, not capable, and not loveable that I felt afraid to let go of these beliefs; who would I be without them? To take on a new set of beliefs where I was telling myself that I was enough and a good and loving person felt alien to me at first. It was like when you first put on a new pair of shoes, and they feel a little uncomfortable for a while until you walk for a bit and get used to them. It felt like I was creating the person I knew myself to be, and I was now taking on the responsibility of healing myself. What sometimes hindered me was that I wanted that healing from my abusers, which would never happen, and I had to give it to myself. My anger towards them both was the thing that kept me stuck at times and reinforced all the negative beliefs I learnt to believe about myself from my abusers and others around me.

In the beginning, the journey ahead felt impossible for me. Impossible that I could heal from all of this, yet the joyful emotions were telling me I could. Those emotions were the guiding light I held under the shadow of my anger and grief around what had happened to me. I resisted seeing that the light of my knowledge and understanding were the keys to giving me the relief I needed to move forward and release me from the prison built around me by my family member's abuse.

The fear of allowing the loving child I was before the abuse to become the loving person I am and to be present in my adult life was the same as that of the abused child in me. There were times I had given my all to my relationships only to end up being hurt deeply. I recognised it as the child in me constantly seeing the good or wanting to see the good in others and denying the pain and hurt they were causing me. Again, this is another pattern that I had learned as a child. It was easier to blame myself, to see myself as the bad, unlovable person than to accept that another had created this for me.

My search had begun with me feeling unhappy, and I continued to do what had been done to me by still believing I was what someone else had thought me to be. I knew I had to change my beliefs and change these patterns.

To question our beliefs about ourselves, we need to ask if what we are thinking or saying to ourselves is true. Is it our voice or another's voice we hear that is directing how and what we believe about ourselves? I realised that my self-talk didn't belong to me; it belonged to the adults in my life and their perception of who I should be in their eyes and how they dismissed my true self. I felt denial of who I was as a child and what had happened to me as that child. Throughout my life, I have made myself invisible to others and mostly to myself. There were so many unconscious beliefs that hadn't even surfaced yet but would continue to surface as I learnt more about myself and the truth around myself as I journeyed forward.

As children, we are like sponges. We take in what our parents say and what other significant adults in our lives say and make what they say our own beliefs and carry them forward into our own lives. One of the beliefs I carried around money was that we were blessed, we had enough, and we were in relation to what others had. A roof over our heads, food on the table, clothes to wear, and access to education. Having these things was enough. They were enough until my dreams came in, and I realised that enough held me in a place where I couldn't dream of something better or outside the parameters of what my parents had taught me to believe. I carried their beliefs around money with me, and in doing so, I had limited what I could earn and who I could help. This belief stifled my happiness by limiting my earnings to being enough when I wanted more for my family and myself.

Another belief I had at that time was to be grateful for what my parents were providing for me and to excuse what behaviours they had that brought me to feeling so bad about myself. I was taught to excuse the pain others may cause me and to look for what they were doing for me in other ways, like providing the needed material things. I longed for more. I longed to be understood, to have my opinions listened to, and even have them challenged instead of accepting my parents' opinions and mostly my father's opinions towards his life and ours.

Now, some thirty years on, and with all the understanding and knowledge I have gained on my journey, I know that healing is possible. When we start on our journey toward our healing, it is the vision we hold for ourselves and why we want to heal that is important. The challenges and the process of that journey lead us to reclaim the lost parts of ourselves and embrace our light and purpose. In the journey, we see the blocks created for us that stop us from having what we want, healing from the limitations that were put upon us, and painting a new image of who we truly are. The freedom I feel now to be myself and speak my truth brings joy to my life and relationships. I am so happy that I stepped onto my path, and even though I resisted at times the changes that I needed to make, I knew I was not only embracing myself more but that my faith and belief in a power greater than me that wanted the best for me.

As you step into your journey, know that there is a guiding light within you that wants the best for you and will guide you to the means to create that life for yourself. When you learn to trust yourself as the wonderful, loving being that you are, you are opening yourself up to allowing the connection and presence of something magnificent into your life and, in doing so, also into the lives of others. We are all connected. No one of us is better than the other. We all have trials and challenges along our paths throughout our lives; how we meet those trials and challenges enables us to heal from our past and step forward to create the lives we dream of. Knowing yourself, understanding the truth of who you are, and honouring your story and journey are your connection with a higher power within your life. Do each day a step towards creating a better life for yourself, and within a year, you will have taken 365 steps to make that life and your dreams more present.

As I look back from the place I am in right now, I can see how those memories were my guiding light to the changes I needed to make within myself and my life. It came from within myself, and with each memory, I learnt to trust more in myself and, in doing so, began to create the life I had dreamed of. Was it all perfect? No. Did I still have my challenges? Yes. The one thing that changed the most was my faith in my God, and my trust in my knowledge also became stronger. My relationships deepened, and I felt at peace within myself.

My hope throughout this book is that I have supported you in some way towards your healing, and in telling you my story, I have given you some skills that enable you to go towards your healing and the guidance to create a better future for yourself. From my heart to yours, and with love and light, I wish the best for you as you journey forward.

Teresa.

Resources

Meditation: Healing the Feeling Within

Find a comfortable chair, feet firmly on the floor, with your palms upwards, or if you prefer, a comfortable space to lie down in.

Begin by taking a breath in and a breath out, breathing into your diaphragm, breathing out through your nose, and allowing your body to relax more and more with each breath.

Now, breathing into your heart and allowing whatever feeling you need to work on right now to come to the fore as you are breathing into your heart. It's a feeling that you have been taught to dismiss, and for now, within your heart, you are allowing it to be with you.

Opening your heart to this feeling allows its presence, love, and compassion to flow from your heart to this feeling. Breathing in love and compassion and breathing out any negative feelings that are surfacing. Allowing the flow of love and compassion towards this feeling. Just allowing it to be as it is.

As you breathe, allow whatever emotions come with this feeling.

Holding love and compassion towards this feeling as emotions arise and allowing the emotions to flow.

Let the feeling speak to you, to bring understanding and a message of healing that will ease this feeling for you. The message might be in the form of a word, image, or a sensation in your body. Keep sending love and compassion towards whatever is arising for you until you can begin to feel an ease within your body. Rest in this ease and allow it to flow from your heart outwards within your body until your body is filled completely with this ease. Stay with this ease for as long as you need to, and when you are ready, connect back with your body from your head all the way down towards your feet and feel your feet connected to the ground beneath your feet. When you are ready and in your own time, open your eyes and connect with the space you are in by looking around you.

Teresa Clifford

Meditation for Healing the Inner Child.

Find some relaxing music to do the meditation with. Make yourself comfortable either lying down or in a sitting position. Breathe into your diaphragm and out through your nose. With each breath you take, scan your body from head to toe and use your breath to ease out any tension you may find in your body. Do this until you are feeling deeply relaxed.

Then, in your mind's eye, take yourself to your favourite place. It could be a garden, a mountain range, or the seaside, wherever brings you joy. When you reach this place within yourself, as you look around, you see yourself as a child and greet them. Please take in what your child is wearing, how it looks, and what it is doing. What is your child's reaction to seeing you? Are they happy that you are there? Do they invite you to play with them? Spend some time with them in whatever way they need you to be with them, chatting and playing with them if that is what is needed. Ask your child if they need or want anything from you right now. Take in what they say and tell them you will follow through on what they have asked.

When you feel it is time to leave, end the conversation with them, letting them know that you are going. They may choose to come with you, or they may choose to stay. Find out what is appropriate for them. If they choose to come with you, take them by the hand and bring them with you. Should they choose to stay, let them know that you will come again to visit them. Connect with your breath again and allow your breath to connect you back with your body, whether sitting or lying down. Please take a few deep breaths, wiggle your fingers, connect with your feet, and bring movement to them. When you are ready, open your eyes and come back into the room. Please take a moment to write about what it was like to be with your child and what has come up for you within the meditation.

Teresa Clifford

Assertiveness

Understanding our rights can aid us in identifying what we want and need. Knowing what we have a right to as a person can highlight how those rights were dismissed in childhood. Here is a list of rights that are yours:

1. I have the right to state my own needs and set my priorities as a person independent of any roles I may assume.
2. I have the right to be treated with respect as an intelligent, capable, and equal human being.
3. I have the right to express my feelings.
4. I have the right to express my own opinions and values.
5. I have the right to say YES and NO for myself.
6. I have the right to make mistakes.
7. I have the right to change my mind.
8. I have the right to say I don't understand.
9. I have the right to ask for what I want.
10. I have the right to decline responsibility for other people's problems.

11. I have the right to deal with others without being dependent on them for approval.

From Anne Dickson's *A Woman in Your Own Right* (1982) Quartet Books Ltd.:London

Saying No assertively

Saying No assertively means using the word 'No' without padding it out, making excuses, or trying to soften the blow.

When someone makes a request, listen to your body language. Is it saying:

1. I don't want this.

2. I am not sure; I need time to think.

3. I am prepared to help but not do exactly as asked.

4. Yes, I want to do this.

If (1), then say 'No, I don't want to… and thank you for asking. If the other person persists in asking, keep repeating yourself without getting into a discussion or taking on responsibility for the other person's problem.

If (2) applies, ask for time to consider your position and say when you will get back to them.

If (3), say, ' I am willing to lend you half the amount you have asked for…', or whatever applies to the situation.

If (4) applies, say, 'Yes, I would like to go out for a drink, or whichever response is relevant in the situation, 'and thank you for asking me.'

Owning our feelings is part of assertiveness

As we come to terms with what triggers us and grasp what those triggers are, we can begin to take responsibility for our feelings. This means then that we have a choice on how we respond to a feeling that is pleasant or one that is unpleasant, and the action we take or how we deal with it. For example, if we feel angry because of something someone said, we are responsible for dealing with that feeling and the person who made the statement. If we fly off the handle, that is our responsibility, and we cannot blame the other person.

In all situations involving adults, we are 100% responsible for our feelings, thoughts, and actions. This is different from when we were the child when the adult involved us as the child in an adult situation. The responsibility lay solely with the adult on how the adult treated us. As adults in an adult situation, both ourselves and the other person involved are 100% responsible for their feelings, thoughts, and actions.

As a child coming from an abusive situation with an adult, we learnt to feel certain feelings and, more importantly, when and how to express those feelings. For this reason, if we feel hurt because of something someone says, their statement has probably triggered a response we learned in childhood. As adults, our responsibility is to deal with these feelings constructively by expressing them openly if we want to and stop blaming others.

The benefit of being assertive and owning feelings is very great. By owning and taking responsibility for our feelings, we can choose how we behave and control our lives. We are likewise not responsible for the other person's feelings, which releases us from many unpleasant consequences in difficult situations, such as guilt, shame, etc.

Assertive Ways of Expressing Feelings

Using words

'I feel… (followed by a 'feeling' word)

'I feel…when…'

'I feel…because…'

Using 'I' statements when expressing our feelings gives us more ownership of our feelings.

Unassertive ways of expressing feelings

Any language that blames the other person is not being assertive, for example:

'You make me feel…'

'I feel that you…'

The difference between expressing feelings assertively is not about blaming the other person, as in –

Making the statement, 'You make me feel…' Or judging the issue as in, 'I feel that you don't like me. This is better said assertively: ' I feel sad because I imagine you don't like me anymore.'

Affirmations for Healing from Trauma

1. Today, I choose me.

2. I do not blame myself for my childhood experiences/trauma.
3. My mind, body, emotions, and spirit belong to me.
4. My life is filled with miracles, especially mine.
5. I am capable of transforming negative experiences into something positive.
6. No one can take my truth away from me; I speak my truth, even if my voice hurts.
7. Every day, I am creating a more meaningful life.
8. I am changing in positive ways. I am making peace with my past and accepting myself.
9. My life is divinely guided.
10. Today, I choose to focus on the things I can control

Affirmations for Trauma by Dr. Robyn Gobin.

My Declaration of Self-Esteem

I am me.

In all the world, there is no one else exactly like me.

Some persons have parts like me, but no one adds up exactly like me.

Therefore, everything that comes from me is authentically mine because I choose it.

I own everything about me

My body, including everything it does;

My mind, including all its thoughts and ideas:

My eyes, including the images of all they behold;

My feelings, whatever they may be…

Anger, joy, frustration, love, disappointment, excitement;

My mouth and all the words that come out of it,

Polite, sweet or rough, correct or incorrect;

My voice, loud or soft;

And all my actions, whether they be to others or myself.

I own my fantasies, dreams, hopes, and fears.

I own all my triumphs and successes (all my failures and mistakes)

I know there are aspects about myself that puzzle me and other aspects that I do not know.

But as long as I am friendly and loving to myself,

I can courageously and hopefully look for solutions to the puzzles and ways to discover more about myself.

However, I look and sound,

Whatever I say and do, and whatever I think and feel at a given moment, is me.

This is authentic and represents where I am at that moment in time.

When I review later how I looked and sounded, what I said and did,

And how I thought and felt, some parts may turn out to be unfitting, and keep that which proved fitting and invent something new for that which I discarded.

I can see, hear, feel, think, say, and do.

I have the tools to survive, to be close to others, to be productive, and to make sense and order out of the world of people and things outside of me.

I own me, and therefore, I can engineer myself.

I am me, and I am okay.

Virginia Satir

www.ingramcontent.com/pod-product-compliance
Lightning Source LLC
Chambersburg PA
CBHW052058110526
44591CB00013B/2263